First You Run, Then You Walk

"Essential reading for anyone seeking a reason to run—whether a mile or a marathon—and seeking to better appreciate the fundamental joy in hard work, fanciful competition, and pumping hard down the home straight. **First You Run, Then You Walk** will nurture both your inner Bannister and your inner Thoreau."

Marc Bloom, award-winning running
journalist, author, and editor

"This eloquent, witty, poignant book captured me from start to finish. I am not a runner, but as a reader I was so captivated by Tom Hart's stories that I entered his world and found myself totally intrigued by both the rituals of running and the moving story of his triumph over adversity."

Doris Kearns Goodwin, Presidential historian/memoirist,
author of *The Bully Pulpit*, *Team of Rivals* and many more

"In these inspiring essays Tom Hart balances a record of ambition and achievement with moving reflections on loss and acceptance. Here is a voice that will stay with us for a long time, simultaneously literary, amusing, and wise."

Lewis Hyde, author of
The Gift, *Trickster Makes This World* and *Common As Air*

"Whether you're a front runner or a plodder, you'll find much to enjoy as you share Tom Hart's personal running (and walking) quests. Hart's style is evocative and lively, and you'll be reminded of the fear, the adrenaline rush, the satisfaction, and the pure fun you've had chasing your own goals."

Don Kardong, Olympic marathoner,
author of ***Thirty Phone Booths To Boston***.

"I found ***First You Run, Then You Walk*** to be a delight. It is well written, witty, and poignant. In the background are themes of obsession, aging, and mortality – in this case made all the more penetrating by a battle with cancer and removal of a lung. All of which makes the book, as all good books are, not only about running but about life."

Alan Lightman, essayist and novelist,
author of **Einstein's Dreams**

"I read Tom Hart's ***First You Run, Then You Walk*** with interest and pleasure and recommend it to any runner or fan of running, or to any fan of good writing, for that matter. Hart has managed to experience and ponder so many different and resonant aspects of the running life, and he renders them with humor, wisdom, and great poignancy."

John L. Parker, Jr., author of
New York Times bestseller ***Once A Runner***

FIRST
YOU RUN,
THEN
YOU WALK

PEDESTRIAN THOUGHTS

TOM HART

Published by:

Tom Hart Books
Concord, Massachusetts

Cover Photo: Tom Hart
Author Photo: Garrett Knight

ISBN: 978-0-9904954-0-6

CONTENTS

ACKNOWLEDGMENTS

I've enjoyed and learned from many other writ-
ers-about-running, starting long ago when I picked up
Joe Henderson's *Run Gently, Run Long* back in the 1970s.
Editor/Writer Marc Bloom was an early supporter of my
essays, and I've had the pleasure of working with Marc in
a variety of ways over the years. From long-ago Riverside,
Connecticut neighbor Jim Fixx through Olympic marathoner and essayist Don Kardong, the list is long, and
would have to include Rich Benyo, John Parker, Kenny
Moore, and my favorite runner/writer of them all, James
Shapiro—and the list still would be incomplete. Running
seems to lend itself to thinking, often with unusual per-
spectives, and reading the works of all of the above, and
others, has educated me as I've been entertained.

My walker/writer models go back a bit further: all of
the English Romantics, especially my particular literary
hero, William Hazlitt, were walkers. Going back further
still, Montaigne was on his feet a lot and not averse to
talking about it. Closer to our time, and much closer to

my Concord, Massachusetts, home was perhaps the all-time walking/writing champ, Henry David Thoreau, with whom I've been carrying on inner arguments for many years.

I was lucky to have begun my running in the Boston area, a nexus of the activity, and to have found my way early to the still-flourishing Cambridge Sports Union, so many of whose members were helpers and role models, none more so than the estimable-in-every-way Rob Riordan. When we moved to Concord and I made a marathoning comeback in 1996 for the 100th Boston, the Concord Runners were a welcoming and helpful group. And certainly coaching for years with Steve Lane at Concord-Carlisle High School was an unparalleled education for me.

My biggest enablers and supporters, of course, have been my immediate family. Becky, Patrick, and Eamonn, my children, have all been runners at one time or another, and beyond that have been my teachers in various ways. And my wife, Christopher, the real writer in the family (and who in her late-blooming rowing has become the athlete in the family as well) is simply the one who makes everything possible.

Thanks, everyone!

for Christopher

. . . — I cannot paint
What I then was. The sounding cataract
Haunted me like a passion: the tall rock,
The mountain, and the deep and gloomy wood,
Their colors and their forms, were then to me
An appetite; a feeling and a love,
That had no need for a remoter charm,
By thought supplied, nor any interest
Unborrowed from the eye. — That time is past,
And all its aching joys are now no more,
And all its dizzy raptures. Not for this
Faint I, nor mourn nor murmur; other gifts
Have followed; for such loss, I would believe,
Abundant recompense. ...

> William Wordsworth, from *Tintern Abbey*,
> (meditating on the old days when he
> could run sub-3:00 marathons)

Prologue

For most of the sixty-odd years of my life, a run of some
sort was part of my days. That's no longer the case, mainly
because the removal of a cancerous lung a few years ago
shortened the range of my longest runs from a couple
of hours to a couple of minutes. I acknowledge myself a
lucky guy, my remaining lung healthy and strong as I live
a life as full of joy as that of a compulsive reader and Red
Sox fan can be.

I am far from being any sort of techie, but I do acknowledge a profound gratitude that I live in the age of
the iPod, and confess that for me the fundamental vehi-
cle for bringing order out of chaos is the playlist. What
follows is a playlist of essays/pieces I hope runners and
walkers alike—and even perhaps a sedentary reader—
will enjoy: my love letter to pedestrianism in all its forms.
Further, I hope runners and walkers alike will see something of their own struggles and joys in mine.

Though there is meant to be a vague sort of
semi-chronological order to this playlist, any of the pieces

should be pleasurable on its own. They share a general tone of welcome. There are pieces here that were originally published decades apart, as well as some that have never been published at all. This is in keeping with the notion that a playlist should exhibit some texture. My driving-tunes playlist, for example, can include, among others, Tracy Chapman's *Fast Car*, Chuck Berry's *You Can't Catch Me*, and Tom Waits's *Looking For the Heart of Saturday Night*, different though those tunes—classics all—are. And different though the chapters that follow may be, they have in common an interest in the quality of attention paid to the value of the ordinary.

For my running, and walking, have been clearly, relentlessly ordinary from the first, and yet they've been of central importance to me throughout my life, especially in my years of adult awareness. You may choose from this playlist the song/essay of a very fit, mid-thirties runner as he tries to break five minutes for a mile on the track, or a chapter about a fellow in his sixties on the hunt for WMDs. (No, not as in Iraq, but rather as in Winning My Division in age-group racing.) The joys of a running journal are on offer in my account of trying to run every day for a year in the early 1980's, and I have a chapter about the wonderfully obscure world of high school cross country, as I experienced it coaching in the 2000s.

In addition to these pieces and other running ruminations, I write about what I've found as, following the removal of my lung, I have made walking rather than running a central daily activity. I've had to struggle with identity issues, after decades of calling myself a runner.

Sometimes there's been a direct running/walking relationship—*all right, I can't run a marathon so I'll go out and
walk 26.2 miles and that'll show 'em!* This directly comparative tone, though, is rare, and walking—once I moved
past my residual runnerly feelings that any walk is a failure simply by virtue of its not being a run—is not always
seen simply as a substitute for something else, but experienced on its own terms. Aerobic fitness is far from my
consciousness, for example, as I wander around in one
chapter making little rock-pile cairn/sculptures in my
Great Meadows National Wildlife Refuge backyard in
Concord, Massachusetts.

So read the chapters, the playlist entries, as you like,
in whatever order, and read into them what you like. My
goals have been to make sharing these experiences with
me enjoyable for you, and for you to see yourself in them
with me. To borrow from my long-ago Concord neighbor and fellow walker Thoreau, in *Walden*: "If I seem to
boast [or simply talk about ME] more than is becoming,
my excuse is that I brag for humanity rather than myself:
and my shortcomings and inconsistencies do not affect
the truth of my statement."

CHAPTER ONE

THE CARDBOARD MILE

*In mechanical efforts, you improve by perpetual practice,
and you do so infallibly, because the object to be attained
is not a matter of taste or fancy or opinion, but of actual
experiment, in which you must either do the thing or
not do it.*

WILLIAM HAZLITT, *The Indian Jugglers*

1981: IN MY MID-THIRTIES, I had no track background, and was curious about what my regular fifty- or sixty-mile weeks might translate to in terms of mile speed. I was fit and full of energy; I felt all things were possible. Certainly I ought to be able to cut down my soft mile track PR (personal best record), since I had none! I'd spent a few years by then running the roads, so getting on a track at all was sure to be something new.

The idea, having simmered in the primordial soup of my subconscious mind for who knows how long, bubbled up full-blown in early June of 1981: I dubbed it The Cardboard Mile. In previous years I had projected, in annual New Year's enthusiasms, breaking five minutes for the mile as one of my yearly running goals. But for a variety of reasons, as other PRs passed away, as I went below twenty-eight minutes for five miles and an hour for ten, five minutes for one mile remained unbroken. Not just unbroken—unexplored. In my mid-thirties, I had never run a single competitive mile.

But this would be the year, this summer. I saw it clearly. Yes, a couple of months of regular track workouts. A new training emphasis. And by the time late August rolled around—why, wasn't there going to be another Golden Mile this year? A summer summit of milers, towards which Steve Scott, Steve Ovett, Sebastian Coe, and the rest would be aiming? Well, then, I thought, I'll aim for late August, too, and my own Big Mile, though perhaps mere cardboard in comparison to their Golden one, would be the focus of *my* summer.

Definitely. A sub-five minute mile. Why not? Later, a number of answers to that question would suggest themselves, but in early June I just let my fantasies roll. . . .

I considered the idea, nestled in my Trailways bus seat, speeding towards my college reunion, the first such I'd attended. Fifteen years: enough to set one musing, to be sure, and I mused the weekend away, alternately picturing myself as a speedy miler and as an over-fed jogger hovering dangerously on the brink of outright middle age. As it happened, I had a chance Saturday afternoon to launch my miling career appropriately at (trumpet flourishes, please) the Alumni Track Meet.

I had noticed this event listed among the reunion activities in the advance material I'd received, and had really been quite looking forward to it. Unrelated as my marathoning might be to any track event, I'd guessed that the likely lack of any serious competition would give me a chance to shine. I actually—by way of serious training— skipped Saturday's lunch to be at the top of my form, such as it was. Thus it was somewhat disconcerting to find, as I jogged over to the track at the appointed hour to loosen up, a mere five or six people milling about aimlessly, none entirely certain what was going on.

After a while a few more people, mostly kids under ten, drifted over, including a member of the college's athletic department, who seemed to be the meet's organizer. After getting the kids' softball throw contest (obviously the real main attraction) underway, he turned his attention to the running events. An undergraduate who'd been enlisted to help out with the reunion weekend was there, in running attire. He turned out to be a member of the college cross country team. Another lanky bystander turned out to be the cross country coach, who agreed to run, too, once it was ascertained that all the alumni runners present were interested in trying a quick mile. I was all the alumni runners present.

The three of us toed the line. A hot June afternoon. The black cinder track. It would doubtless have brought back memories of athletic trials and triumphs of the past, except that I'd never run track or cross country at any level in school. This was to be my first race at the distance.

I bolted into the lead, feeling smooth and easy. The kid couldn't be in racing shape, I figured, and the coach had said he was racing the next day and was just along for the ride. He pulled into the lead after about 200 meters, though, and through the first lap we were pretty well bunched at 75 seconds. Hey, I thought to myself, right on five-minute pace, and this isn't so bad. I'm looking at a 4:50 easy once I get the work in.

The undergraduate passed me during the second lap, and as we went through the half I trailed them by just a second or two in what someone called out as 2:32. I was working hard by now, my early enthusiasm ebbing fast.

It disappeared entirely during the third lap, as my two opponents pulled farther away, due more to my slowing, I'm sure, than to any speeding up on their part. I missed the three-lap split, desperately trying to regain some contact, failing, embarrassed that the by-now huge crowd of ten or twelve should be witnesses to this debacle. Such coherent thoughts as I could muster touched on whether any of the crowd might be able to give me the medical attention I'd need when I collapsed. How had my pride led me to this spotlight of disgrace!

I gave my ultimate effort in that last lap, trying not to let the large gap between me and the leaders grow larger still. They cruised in with steady times, both at 5:02. I staggered across in 5:07, utterly spent. Five seconds is NOT contact in a mile race, I found out. This miling

4

business isn't so easy after all, I thought, once I'd been able to take in enough oxygen to think at all. Ouch.

Still, I reflected the next week, as I tried to put that painful experience into its proper perspective, it was a beginning. And with the physical agony fading into more-manageable memory, I allowed myself to think it was not so bad a beginning, at that. It had, after all, given me a reference point, a mile race, a time I could improve.

My scheming became intense. Always one who enjoys the planning, calculating aspects of training (when everything seems so possible), I soon had a schedule mapped out that seemed right. It differed from other serious training periods I'd planned, build-ups for target marathons, in one major respect: it ignored mileage. I aimed for three faster workouts (or two fast workouts and one short race), around three "rest" days of five to seven easy miles, plus one day's run getting into the thirteen-to-fifteen mile range. It was quite a concession to realize that this meant my mileage would never get much above fifty for any week during the plan. Years of legitimizing my training by counting mileage totals had to be forgotten. Quality, not quantity, mattered now. The only problem was, I didn't know much about quality track workouts.

One thing I did know was that I'd need support for my plan, and luckily I was able to convince two friends to aim for the Cardboard Mile with me. We agreed we'd try to work out together on the track at least once a week.

I meticulously projected various workouts, elaborately detailing how fast we would run our 200- 300-, or 400-meter sets, how we'd mix distances. Something in me responded rapturously to the intricate number games. I could almost sense myself becoming fitter, faster, just scribbling the numbers: Gee, if I can run 10 x 300 meters all between 51 and 54 seconds, then surely a five-minute mile is in the bag.

Well, maybe. Of course, writing up progressively tougher workouts and running those workouts are very different things, the latter considerably more difficult. But at the very least, moving to interval workouts offered the benefit of achieving, in one day's running, many small goals, as well as a qualitatively different athletic experience. I could obsess about running again in ways I hadn't for some years. I had returned to a state of running innocence, and relished this start of a new phase of my running life.

We gathered for our first joint speedwork session, meeting after work at the M.I.T. track. What a day we'd chosen to begin! At 6:00 PM, the temperature still hovered near 90, with humidity at a sopping high. Steve arrived last, moaning already. He, Rob, and I agreed a gentle initial workout was in order, if we could figure out what that meant in the strange context of this ultramodern (no cinder here, thank you) red oval track.

As we did some warm-up laps, we noticed a good many kids, from what looked like grade-schoolers all the way up to college-age, doing some sort of group workout. Every so often a small bunch would tear past us, looking fast and smooth. Intimidating. Here we were, hardened road racers about to strut our stuff, watching these kids zip by.

That's one of the things about track work. The lone-
liness of the long distance runner doesn't come into play
here. In the limited space of the 400-meter track, even
while one isn't paying real attention to other runners,
there's an awareness of what's going on all around. It's
hard to fantasize about being an Olympian when you
have to be prepared to yield your lane to the "Track!"
command of someone steaming by much faster.

We did a last loosening lap, then hit our watches passing the line into our first 400 meters. I felt great. We'd
begun! And, whether it was because it was so hot and we
were therefore extra-loose, or because we wanted to look
good for the other tracksters there, we rolled through that
first 400 meters in 68 seconds. *Okay!*

Okay! became *Okay?* as I struggled for breath checking my watch and gasped out what Rob, who'd caught
me at the end, and I both knew: *Too fast!* My fastest ever,
in fact, impossible to sustain, and sustaining, managing,
is exactly what's at the core of speedwork. Steve, who'd
lagged on our first lap, led us through the second in a
much-more-reasonable 71 seconds, but a hard lesson had
been dealt us. We had to begin the learning of sub-max-
imal speediness.

A couple of 2:34 800s, pretty evenly paced, were followed by two more 400s, in 76 and a final 74 seconds. A
beginning, and particularly given the heat, we all left the
track that evening feeling quite virtuous. And there *was*
that 68-second lap—though I wouldn't have felt quite so
dazzled by that had I known it would be the fastest lap I'd
run all summer.

Note to myself, early July: Ran a 4:37 mile yesterday. Very exciting, but I have to confess it was done in sections, with rests between: 200s in 33 and 34 seconds, 400s in 71 and 72, then two more 200s in 33 and 34. Presto—4:37!

This is what interval training is all about, it seems. The point is, how can you expect to run under five minutes (or six, or four) for a mile unless you've *practiced* running that fast? And if you can't do it in the first place, how can you practice? There's a clear Catch-22 involved here, but you can get around it. You simply run that fast (or faster) but for shorter distances. Accustoming yourself to the pace over eighths, quarters, and halves, you build the capacity to sustain it over a mile. Simple, right?

Note to myself, late July: Trouble. Almost a month and a half into my new program designed to bring me to super speediness, I'm overweight, undertrained, and probably further from being able to run a sub-five-minute mile than I was at my reunion. I seem to have somehow blown it, and—for the record—I ought to try to see just how.

First and foremost, I rushed things. I plunged right into tough workouts, and after a couple of weeks had bashed myself into tendon injuries that kept me from running at my best during this crucial training period. Whether because, as the organizer of this quixotic quest, I'd felt the need to shine, or simply due to some innate competitiveness, I'd pushed too hard. That ridiculous-in-retrospect opening 68-second 400 turned out to have been symbolic. All-important lesson number one: Track workouts are not races, and should not be run at top speed.

Furthermore, I'd overlooked an undeniable, and crucial, fact. The rest of my life had gone on, had not been bypassed by my new running priorities. Thus, for example, entertaining the in-laws through the first weeks of July left me with a *bon vivant's* silhouette instead of the leaner frame I'd counted on in my initial enthusiasm. Mr. Willpower I'm not.

It would surely have been useful to have known more about the theory and practice of speedwork when this thing began. Looking back, I'd have advised myself to start more slowly, but with the aim of doing what are called quality intervals, the kind designed to build speed, rather than stamina, through repeats of fast work with enough rest between them to recover and do the next hard portion at high-quality levels. I have to add, decades later, and having done quite a bit of coaching during that time, that circuit exercising to build core body strength and stretching and drills to help range of motion would have been very helpful.

In any case, I was learning by experience, and there were still a few weeks before the Cardboard Mile. I might be able to regroup somehow and still pull it off.

Aching legs propped up on my flimsy porch railing, I gazed idly over the boxy back yards and slanted roofs of my Somerville neighborhood, quaffing a cold beer on a warm August evening, thoroughly disgusted with myself. My running was flat, lifeless. I was wiped out.

I pondered the almost monastic dedication, the life of discipline that top milers (or top athletes of any kind) must undertake. There was something seductive about it, as I imagined. Once one made the commitment, there would always be an answer to whatever conflict or question arose. Since the first principle was clear—Everything Is About Helping My Running—one could move forward without doubts, without hesitations. Perhaps, like the great Aussie miler Herb Elliot or Japanese marathon sensation Toshihiko Seko, one even had a guru-coach who outlined one's entire waking day.

Seductive, perhaps, in a way, but also manifestly impossible for me, Mr. Middle-aged book editor, and, therefore, in the end, merely depressing. A dramatic improvement in my own times wouldn't be accomplished as easily as I'd imagined. There were levels of discipline and sacrifice beyond what I was prepared to put up with. I had a new dimension of respect for the elite star runners, who, it seemed, were less like the rest of us than I'd thought.

It was hard, but I had to admit to myself, as I finished my beer, that for all my fantasies about new intense training this summer, my paltry efforts, limited as they were, would make those *real* runners laugh.

But here the road of my ruminations split, and I saw a second possibility. The road of excellence-through-discipline made running the standard by which the rest of one's life is measured. But I saw there was another road, too—a much more worn road, at that. It offered other, more familiar satisfactions. All sorts of runners, even (gasp) joggers, used this road, and on it there was no distinction admitted between real and less-than-real runners. There were only people, people running. I was as real a runner as I needed to be, and I knew that in a few weeks I'd run a good hard mile, and that, whatever the time, somehow the whole experience would be worth the trouble. And knowing that, I creaked up out of my chair and shuffled back into the kitchen to crack open another beer, despite what Sebastian Coe might have thought.

The day before the Big Attempt my discipline was sterner: no beer, very light eating, early to bed. I'd made some calls over the past few days, and it appeared that the Cardboard Mile would have a reasonable field, including a speedster or two capable of times in the 4:40's or even below, the intrepid three of us who'd pointed towards this together, and a few other fellow runners who'd been around five minutes in the past but weren't too sure about what kind of mile shape they might be in currently.

My final calculations had been thought out. I had to begin with what I knew I could do, and what I knew I could do (this *knowing* as important a result of the track sessions as the actual physical ability) was to go through the first quarter in 73 seconds and continue. After that, things got cloudy, though I knew I'd have to leave myself some leeway, gain myself a few seconds over the first half. That meant a second quarter of not over 75 seconds after my opening 73, for at least a 2:28 split. Then I hoped to use the people in front of me (and I was quite sure there *would* be people in front of me) to pull me through a third quarter in 76 or 77 seconds, thus leaving me a decent shot of going below five minutes if only I could muster a 75-second final lap.

God, what would that last lap be like? Finding that out was one of the main mysteries of this whole endeavor.

I'd read and re-read not only training materials but also books describing the experience of running the mile. Some of the best were fiction: *The Olympian* by Brian Glanville, *Once a Runner* by John Parker. In the Parker book someone says that where the real supreme effort is needed is on the early part of the last lap, that "everyone has heart going down the stretch." I was prepared to project a gut-busting final 100-200 meters, but what about the third lap and the first half of the last one? *Terra Incognita.*

When in doubt, play with numbers. Anyone who derives great enjoyment from meticulous planning for a marathon will be delighted to learn that attacking the mile distance can offer just as many opportunities to plan and project. And considerable spice is added when you realize that, in a mile, there's a good deal less margin for error. Instead of torturing—happily, of course—over calculations involving miles, or groups of miles, you are projecting split times over 400, 200, even 100 meters. If your plan calls for a 72-second split for 400 meters and you go through 200 more than a second or two from 36, you're in trouble! By extension, if your first 100 meters for that lap takes you, say, 20 seconds, then already disaster looms.

I finally managed to tighten up the calculations so precisely that it became clear that this would be like no road race I'd ever run. The concentration, the attention I'd have to pay, would lead to the qualitatively different running I'd hoped for from the start. Whatever happened, this was definitely going to be something new.

August 13: We gather at the M.I.T. track, with which Rob, Steve and I can now claim some real familiarity. Eight runners have assembled: some pushers, some pullers, and we three, hoping to be pushed, pulled, and otherwise motivated and enabled to our fastest mile times. It's a sultry Thursday evening, and a pretty stiff breeze that will be coming at us as we push up the homestretch bodes ill. I've lined up a starter who will also give us quarter-mile times, and have also recruited someone to call out splits as we pass the half-lap spot. The Cardboard Mile, the main event of our running summer, is really about to happen, and I feel that, at least as a race organizer, I'm a success.

We nervously complete our separate warm-up routines, and are—we hope—ready. *Why don't I feel as fast as these guys look?* But there's no time left to brood, we're called to the line. The other runners at the track sense that something's up, and some pause to watch. We take deep breaths. We're off.

I'm in front again, on the rail and around the first turn to a conservative 20-second opening 100 meters, taking quick comfort from knowing we've accelerated and are moving faster by now. At 200 meters we're timed at 37 seconds, and the fast guys move past to begin their own race, to see who'll win this thing. Fine by me, as I try to stay close behind and run relaxed. I'm after something else. Great! I'm through the first lap in a perfect 73, feeling good. Rob and Steve are right together just in front of me, with the leaders only a stride or two ahead of them.

I make myself think, as I'd planned to, how easy that had seemed compared to the final quarter of 72 seconds

I'd pushed myself through at my last interval workout the preceding Sunday afternoon. Positive imaging, mental strength. Yes, I'm fine, yes, it's working.

Steadily, steadily we run. Incredibly, it all unfolds in what seems like slow motion. I go through 600 meters in 1:50, a perfect 37-second split for that 200 meters, and hold for a 75-second second lap and a half-mile of 2:28. OK, OK, it's fine. I'm holding contact with Steve, who's being pulled along in Rob's wake. The two leaders are by now maybe three seconds clear of Rob, and what's behind me I ignore.

I try so hard to relax during the third lap— which seems to last forever—that I miss the mid-lap split. The leaders are now at least ten seconds in front of me, probably more, and I have only the most tenuous contact with Steve, who's got what looks like three seconds on me. At the three-quarter: 3:46. Damn! I've fallen a second behind five-minute pace!

But I can't panic, and I try simply not to lose any speed, to keep form. A whole lap is too long for a frenzied effort. This at least I've learned. Wait, I tell myself, wait, stride, flow. Don't go for it too soon. After the summer I know just how big this track really is.

And now I'm on the last turn, with less than 200 meters to go. I churn around it, and I know it's time. I make the commitment, pull out all the stops. I'm 100 meters from the end, saving nothing, head bobbing, arms flailing, past embarrassment. My vision has shrunken down to a narrow corridor ahead of me: I see Steve's back, white lines, the red track. Knowing I can't catch him, I'm running harder than I ever have before, trying to catch him anyway. *Pump* hope. *Drive* hope. Fifty meters, 30, 20 and he's across, then I am, too, jabbing frantically at my watch even as I hear it: 4:59. And I can stop.

We did it.

My watch says 4:59.22. I stare at it, savoring each digit. Then I lunge toward Steve (4:57), hug him, and we lurch ahead to Rob (4:51), babbling animatedly. The winner, I learn, finished in 4:43, and number two ran 4:45. One of my pursuers dropped out after a 2:29 half, the others hung in for times of 5:07 and 5:10. We're all happy as little kids at a birthday party, jogging around, trading stories of our experiences, each with his unique version even though we all ran the same four laps. The story for the winner is pulling ahead with 200 meters to go on his victorious kick. The story for Rob is his near-miss on getting below 4:50. Had he been too cautious early? There's a camaraderie, a feeling of shared enterprise, that makes us all reluctant to leave this place where we've done. . .each knows what, each differently.

A month later The Cardboard Mile, all that summer track work, was history, and I was left wondering if there was any neat meaning to be extracted from it all. Was I a "better" runner now that I'd run one mile at about the pace Bill Rodgers went for over 26 of them the previous April in his 2:10:36 Boston Marathon? Certainly, there was a great deal of satisfaction in having achieved a goal I'd wanted to reach for some time. The changed emphasis in my training was sometimes refreshing and always instructive, if also sometimes discouragingly difficult.

Mile racing imposes a radically different physical consciousness, and to try out that consciousness was for me a wonderful experience. Beyond that—hard to say.

On the door of that common household shrine, our refrigerator, are stuck various notes, postcards, cartoons, and other icons. Among them is a fine picture of Sebastian Coe, running almost but not quite directly at the camera, alone, head back and neck muscles tight, driving to the finish line of the 1981 Golden Mile at Brussels. There is no caption, but a small strip of yellow paper has been taped to the lower left-hand corner of the picture. It bears the legend: 4:59.22.

CHAPTER TWO

ROGER BANNISTER AND ME

. . . running − the total, exalted, painful, glorious, miserable, purifying, filthy, rhythmic, dreamy, transcendent, achy experience − for the most part defies rendition in words.

GARTH BATTISTA, EDITOR,
THE RUNNER'S LITERARY COMPANION

THE ALL-THINGS-ARE-POSSIBLE RUNNER OF MY mid-thirties, featured in the previous chapter, isn't to be found here, as I review early athletic inadequacies and much more recent limiting developments. Weaknesses large and small are available to us at all ages, it seems....

Never having been particularly athletic, or physically gifted, I was surprised—very pleasantly so, I must say—to find one day, when I was ten years old, that I'd run a mile in just over four minutes.

Admittedly, there are some aspects of this remembered experience that are, well, let's just say *somewhat sketchily recalled* now, well over half a century later. Perhaps—oh all right, I'll come right out with it—perhaps even unverifiable as hard fact! But I can still conjure the sense of wonder I got at seeing the kitchen clock reading 3:05 as I entered our house, after having energetically jogged all the way home from the Riverside elementary school that fifth-grade afternoon. And had not the school's large clock, set high on the facing above the entrance to the new gym wing, been just gone past three o'clock as I left that day? Clearly, my amazed ten-year-old brain calculated, I'd spent only a little more than four minutes getting home. Wow, pretty darned good!

This would have been (I'm pretty sure I'm right about the fifth-grade dating) in the spring of 1955, and even a relatively dull suburban lad of that era might well have somehow taken in the worldwide uproar about a four-minute mile, peaking the previous year as the elusive feat was finally accomplished by the great Roger Bannister in May of 1954. Track in general, and running a mile in particular, have perhaps never again been as pervasively popular, paid as much attention to, as at that time. Even without yet having become the sports-page junkie I've been for most of my life, I had then, though only a grade-school non-athlete, some rough sense of what a fast mile was.

Aside from my glow of satisfaction that day, I also recall knowing, even then, that there was something not altogether *legitimate* about this particular athletic achievement. I reckoned the distance from my house to my school at about a mile, but knew that my estimate was probably less than one-hundred percent accurate. (But, hey, even if the distance was a bit short, what about the little hill as I turned onto Riverside Avenue after Spruce Street, or even the little hill-let on Jones Park itself, up past the Pearsons' house, in my last stretch? Didn't I have it harder therefore than runners on a flat track? Shouldn't that be taken into account?) Also, I dimly recognized that my timing system wasn't, truthfully, as, well, *precise* as might be desired.

Perhaps most amazing to me was the definite knowledge that *I could have gone faster.* I mean, my little-guy trot had been under control all the way, though I knew that, once I turned onto Jones Park and realized I'd come all that way without walking, I'd picked up the pace a bit for my last quarter-mile, and certainly had raced up the driveway and turned hard to bound up the six stairs to the back door opening onto the breakfast nook at the back end of the kitchen. I'd developed an *interest* in this run of mine about halfway home, I guess, somehow sensing that today I was doing something I hadn't done before.

I must have left school book-less that day, and, perhaps under the spell of a particularly lively and free afternoon air, free of hand and mind, simply wanted to move along at a faster clip than a regular walk. I may have wanted to get home earlier than usual for some reason, but I can't say for sure about that. In any case, there I went, beyond the school grounds and right over the railroad bridge, right up Summit for a couple of hundred yards or so then left onto Spruce—and I suppose unimpeded by fellow school-leavers and luckily not needing to wait for cars when turning or crossing streets. Moving along nicely, feeling good—I was a thoughtless, healthy, happily-trotting little ten-year-old. Then, right onto Riverside Avenue itself, almost immediately the aforementioned slight rise, rewarded by a following slight downhill and then a capacious roadside as the road wound its way curving right, going past St. Paul's Church and thence to Jones Park itself, where I turned left onto the maple-lined corridor with a growing sense of determination and purpose.

Gee whiz! Four minutes and change. I was breathing hard, for sure, and happy to pour myself a glass of (Kool-Aid? lemonade? orange juice? milk? I forget.) as well-earned reward. But really, what kind of a time might I have achieved under better conditions, perhaps having even "trained" somehow? Gosh, what kind of a running marvel *was* I, anyway?

Not much of one, as it turned out. At least, not by any measurable standard. At my elementary school's Field Day activities, I never came close to winning any of the dashes that formed the running events. Smaller and younger than classmates, I never stood out in any way in kickball, or any similar sporting activities. Today's world of all-inclusive organized athletic leagues for youth

soccer, baseball, and so on was unknown at the time—
and that was doubtless lucky for my fragile self-esteem. A
few kids I knew played "little league" baseball, but most
of us contented ourselves with neighborhood games of
SPUD or Hide and Seek or Cowboys and Indians.

I do recall having some positive self-regard for my
abilities in what I called to myself "woods running,"
which meant dodging about solo in nearby woods, jogging instead of simply walking, for no special reason at
all. Perhaps if my school had boasted a Woods Running
team I'd have wanted to try it, but my elementary school,
like all elementary schools in the mid-fifties, had no
sports teams of any kind. These I first encountered when
moving up to Eastern Junior High School in the fall of
1956. I don't remember any fall teams at all, but I know
there was a basketball team, where kids who were unlike
me (good at sports? big?) entertained the rest of us, battling in the gym a few times a year with kids from a
nearby town.

In eighth grade I went off to prep school, where sports
were mandatory every afternoon for everyone. This
healthy policy allowed me to fully comprehend my own
athletic inadequacies, as I participated there, in various
seasons and during various years, in intramural soccer,
wrestling, basketball, tennis, and even crew, with consistent mediocrity. There was no cross country team,
no track team. I was able to utilize my (still strangely
unrecognized) gift for distance running occasionally,
though. When one was late to a meal at this school, one
was sent off by a sixth form (senior) boy authority figure

to "Run the Triangle" before one was admitted to eat. The Triangle consisted of a road running out from the main campus (and refectory) past some athletic fields, a turn onto another road for another few hundred yards, then a last turn back along a driveway that ran past the fields again and ended up back in the school's center. A little short of a mile, I'd guess, and one had the incentive to get through it reasonably efficiently so that one could eat a little something at the end. Get back too late, and the meal was definitely over! But training this wasn't, nor competition.

In college, in a final fruitless spasm of team-sport par- ticipation, I played freshman soccer, mainly watching my very-talented teammates roll to an undefeated season while playing minimally myself. Occasional long team runs (around the campus perimeter, perhaps a mile at most) before practice became for me the chance to show I could keep up, since for the regular players it represented a dull hardship before their playing fun, and as such a part of practice in which they had little or no investment. Thus I was able to finish among the first group most times we did this, furthering my private illusion that I was OK at this running thing, but never leading me to say *hey, I should look into the cross country team instead of this soccer stuff.* Instead I just stopped sports after that first fall season and concentrated on drinking beer. For good measure, and to achieve maximum koolitude—it was 1962, after all, and who knew?—I started smoking.

By the beginning of 1976, I was ready to give up smoking, and shortly after I managed that, I sort of spontaneously broke into a trot one day walking the streets of Cambridge, Massachusetts. That felt good, and led to more trotting, to buying a pair of Adidas running shoes, to still more trotting, and pretty soon, no pioneer I, I'd joined the mass movement of the mid-seventies towards running.

The basic unit of comprehension, the universal coin of the running realm, was and is the mile. Beginning runners, if they turn the corner at all to consciously thinking about their activity, do so by considering issues like: how far am I running? (How many miles?) How fast am I running? (How fast for each mile?) Whether or not one uses this data in a comparative fashion or just to understand one's own actions, it eventually takes the form, mental or material or both, of noting down miles run and when or how they get run.

The mile is something everyone knows, an event run at every high school track meet, a distance understood on every continent. (And I'm not getting sidetracked by any kilometers-miles issues here. Sixteen hundred meters is a mile. Convert if necessary.) Even these days, when I'm walking rather than running, and keeping track by time is much easier, I end up figuring miles, a calculation made easier in many cases because my pedestrian routes echo my familiar former running ones.

Indeed, I marked as a special day during the winter of 2009 the first time in months my daily walk could actually complete a route formerly counted among my regular running stretches. It was, gloomily enough, a three-mile course that included the nearby cemetery, a plowed-sidewalks route useful while the woodsy trails in the Great Meadows National Wildlife Refuge that we border, my regular route, were snowed under and impassable in spots. Though not an especially dear running route, the cemetery loop had been a regular one, and for me to cover it again, albeit at a walk rather than a run, was indeed an important step.

After a January operation to remove my cancerous lung, my walks had begun with short indoor perambulations—five minutes was my first routine. Ours is not a large house, and walking for ten seconds in a straight line from any point will bump you against a wall. A route circling the coffee table in our living room, then heading down a short hall and turning into a bedroom, then back out (after executing a nifty spin move turn) and down same hall, left through kitchen, then circling the round dining-area table and back to the living room took maybe thirty to forty seconds. After seven or eight iterations of that, sometimes varying by— are you ready for it?—*reversing direction for the living room loop*, I could hunker down again to my (re)readings of heaps of hard-boiled detective novels, which for some reason formed a staple of my literary diet for my first month home.

My five-minute treks grew to ten, even beginning to include trips downstairs (two six-stair sections to get there; one does count such things at these times) to meander around the downstairs rooms before the arduous climb back up. Soon I was boldly venturing up another flight of steps (thirteen now) to the big upstairs room, and it may have still been January when I actually bundled up and walked up our short driveway to the mailbox—outside again! Then around our street, and maybe a week after that, in February, pushing on all the way up (and I *felt* the tiny hill) to Bedford Road. I was, at sixty-five, getting used to life with just one lung. And it wasn't so bad. I was a lucky fellow who had inadvertently been preparing for this by decades of cardiovascular exercise, so while I was happy to be expanding my horizons, I didn't consider my February walks miraculous. By March I was getting outside for daily rambles of close to an hour (which translated to about three miles), and noticing that my single lung could savor the occasional tang of spring in the air as well as two.

At some point, as the weather improved, I almost unconsciously started moving my feet slightly faster—*very* slightly, believe me—and found myself, whether under the influence of some especially-sprightly tune from my iPod earbuds or simply in response to the day's soft blandishments, doing what some might almost call *jogging*. Of course I couldn't sustain anything beyond my walk pace for long, but I was mightily intrigued. I tried it again, consciously, on that very walk, and then again a few times over the following days.

In early April I made the discovery that biking was possible—easy around-town biking, that is, on my tame commuting-bike clunker. I find noted in my journal from around then the following: *biked c. 3m to the track at Emerson Field, then walked & jogged a timed mile. Not impressive: just over sixteen minutes!* I admit to real disappointment here. I'd expected a pokey time, of course, but had thought that might mean twelve or thirteen minutes. I'd have thought that sixteen minutes would be a good, up-tempo *walk*, and here I'd done my trotting for a minute or more each lap. I mean, I know I'm around a twenty-minute-per-mile dawdling walker, so my "hard" effort pieces were saving me around, what, a minute per lap? Was that the best I could do?

Not for me now the four-minute mile! No, for me, we now had the four-minute *quarter* mile ....

My rusty running-thought wheels ground into action as slowly as my feet. Hmmm.... what was I supposed to *do* about this? My armada of doctors didn't seem to mind my experimenting. Mainly, though generally approving, they didn't seem terribly interested in details. But details were just what I, on the other hand, couldn't get away from. I seemed to be able to run gently for about two minutes without feeling much physical distress, but when I stopped running and walked on, I experienced shortness of breath and thumping of heart as though I'd just finished a five-mile race.

As spring turned to summer, I began doing three or four walks a week during which, dressed for running, I built in regular intervals of my trotting, trying to learn by observing pattern and progress. My old coaching inclinations told me that if I could train up two lungs, I ought to be able to train up just one to improve, too. In early June one day's journey around the main Great Meadows loop (a little short of two flat, dirt-road miles) took me just under twenty-five minutes, in almost-equal chunks of running and recovery of about a minute and a half each. With the walk over onto the main loop there and the walk back from it, my whole "workout" for the day extended to about thirty-five minutes—noticeably shorter than my usual daily walks, but with much more seriously-focused energy expenditure.

I found I liked it better (as did my wife and frequent training partner, Christopher) when the overall outing lasted longer, with longer rests, and found that the longer rests, plus walking on trails where there were occasional helpful features (read: downhill stretches), enabled me to push my running beyond two minutes by a tiny bit. One giddy July morning I notched a 2:30 stretch. What an achievement! But by late July, my zeal to re-become a runner had lost momentum, for a couple of reasons.

First, this was because the ceiling of something over two minutes seemed locked in. Two, or even two and a half, minutes at a time of running just wasn't impressive enough to me. I always told the girls I coached on our school's cross country team that the work they are putting in today isn't going to be apparent tomorrow, or even next week, that only after about two weeks does one begin to experience any real training effect. Put in the work, you get better: ironclad guarantee, but you have to wait a bit for results to begin showing up.

My lack of measurable improvement after a couple of weeks led me to speculate that for a one-lunged person, it might logically take twice as long as for the two-lunged person to see results, a plausible if probably untrue notion that allowed me to postpone self-chastisement as two weeks of conscious "training" crept up to a month. By

late July my "program" had been in place for well over
two months, and the idea of running, say, an entire mile
without walking still seemed quixotic at best. I certainly
didn't expect to re-enter the marathoning ranks, but I'd
forsaken that field years before, in any case, after dragging
myself through the 100th Boston Marathon in my early
fifties as a goodbye to 26.2 mile efforts. But if I couldn't
do even a single mile, the basic unit, was I really able
to say I was capable of actual running? Maybe I simply
wasn't a runner any more? A question of self-definition I
didn't like thinking about.

My second momentum-losing factor was a jump in my
PSA numbers and a suspicious urological exam that led
to a biopsy and diagnosis with a second kind of cancer,
prostate cancer. The month surrounding the biopsy was
a crash course via readings and consultations (both with
my many doctors and with my many *many* friends who
have prostate cancer) so Christopher and I could assimi-
late and somewhat understand all sorts of possibilities and
consequences. My father had actually died from metasta-
sized prostate cancer, and at just about my age. But I'd put
that down to his too-late diagnosis, and had myself been
vigilant, and (it seemed now entirely too) self-congrat-
ulatory about that vigilance. Twenty-five years after his
death, in today's much better-informed prostate cancer
world, friends of mine who were diagnosed in timely
fashion had all seemed to get through it fine.

But talking to these guys now, really paying attention to them, made it clear that their "getting through it"
had been more arduous than I'd understood: discomfort,

incontinence, impotence. It seemed that, with most treatments, I'd possibly be experiencing more lifestyle change than I'd had to with the lung stuff! I'd been, without meaning to be one, a sort of cancer snob— hey, lung cancer, baby, that's the Big C! I got through that, I'm the man. But what I learned in my crash course in prostate cancer showed me that there can be no cancer snobbery. There is only the disease, always ugly, and the work of getting through it. Which task doesn't ever end.

Luckily—especially as this is not at all intended to be a book about cancer—the biopsy, while positive, was about as good as it could be. Only two of the twelve samples taken showed any cancer at all, and what there was was so small and early that the diagnosticians could only crank up a Gleason score* of 6, and all involved—and at Massachusetts General, doctoring is definitely a team, not an individual, sport— felt that "watchful waiting" was the way to go. Doubtless colored by feeling that I'd had enough medical fun in the last year, we agreed to do nothing at all, actively. We'd keep an eye on things. Lovely!

But I'd had to re-configure my life a bit in anticipation of possible treatments, for example bailing out on the part-time coaching I'd planned to do in the fall. A lot of energy had been expended wrestling with the prostate stuff, and by the time I could try my walk/run training regularly again, in September, I just didn't feel like it. After all, September meant Fall, which would soon

---

* Gleason scores derive from combining two 1-5 ratings applied to sample tissues, lower numbers being better. 7's are pivotal, and anything above 7 generally warrants intervention treatments.

enough drift into—gulp—Winter. Winter has never been this normal New Englander's best running season.

At a September cross country meet I chatted with Newton South's supercoach Steve McChesney, whose teams had battled my Concord-Carlisle girls in friendly fashion and mutual respect for fifteen years, and we talked, among other things, about his younger brother Kenny, who had also lost a lung—and who was running again! *Yeah, he's doin' alright; he had to hold up and wait for me when we last ran together,* Steve told me. Quickly setting aside the fact the Kenny had been an Olympic-caliber runner and was probably twenty years my junior, I perked up my ears. This led to a useful e-mail exchange with Kenny, which was most inspirational, despite the absence of any special training tips.

Also in September, after breaking into my all-too-occasional shuffle one day, I had the feeling that I'd been able, surprisingly, to do a stretch as long as my usual longer ones, but without feeling it as much. I tried out another trot the next day, with a similar feeling that it had been a pretty long one. I'd been wearing no watch, having gotten away from my more conscious "training," but I'd gotten from one regularly-passed gate to the end of that stretch just fine, where before I'd strained to do so on most workouts. Next was noticing that I could go for a whole song or more in my iPod. Finally I timed myself one day, worked it hard, and hit *six minutes*. Wow! Something had changed.

Christopher volunteered the weather as a reason; we'd peaked at two-plus minutes in the heat and humidity of

July. I thought it was that I must be going more slowly, even if that seemed next to impossible given how slowly I'd been going before. The fact that I was eight months past my operation rather than four or five also was given some credit.

Let's see. What if I waited *another* eight or nine months, until next summer even, and could find a way to go even *slower?* Would that allow me to sustain my torpid trot pace for an entire mile? Maybe working towards some sort of goal around that would infuse my running with the kind of conscious energy it had so often shown before. At the next summer's "Adro Mile" (a track and cross country team fund-raising event named for a gifted young scholar-athlete, Adrian Martinez, who'd tragically died just after graduating from college), perhaps I could make it four times around the track. A big point of this newly-begun event was offering miles for everyone, the entire range of runner possibilities. They featured even a mile for anyone who had never run a mile. Hey, maybe they'd have a category that would work for me: 65 and over one-lunged runners with at least two different cancers!? Oh yeah, guys, bring it on.

I thought about how many of my peak running experiences had come from having some sort of a goal, a plan. This make-it-through-an entire-mile thing could give me the focus to somehow re-incorporate running into my life in a more purposeful fashion. And the general method seemed clear: lower expectations and go for it. My fundamental credo! Embracing the ordinary all over again.

Whatever infusion of energy this sort of plan might give me, it had another very positive aspect. It would allow me to coddle myself through the winter, rationalizing that not doing much running was part of my rest plan. I'd continue to walk, of course, and try to do some easy cross-country skiing. Hey, I was sure I'd feel bouncy enough sometimes to try some trotting, even in the snow. But I could postpone any serious work towards running my mile until the spring rolled around. All training is built on the principle of alternating stress and rest, after all, and this plan promised me plenty of rest through the foreseeable future. I'd be in a holding pattern through the winter and then, as spring bloomed, so would my training, in harmony with the world around me. Perfect! The nobility of a goal without the responsibility of (immediately) achieving it. What could be better?

In retrospect, I can see that my operating method here was exactly like that of my running salad days, and that offered a pleasing continuity: I'd found a (theoretically) reachable goal, and experienced immediately how the gratification of thinking about the goal was as good as the accomplishing of it. The benefits of creating a plan don't begin only when that plan is achieved! Thus, even while I wasn't running at all, I could unconsciously consider myself a runner still, one on the injured reserve list, perhaps, temporarily inactivated, but a runner—yes!

CHAPTER THREE

A Foolish Consistency

A man should not rivet himself too fast to his own humours and temperament. Our chief talent is the power of suiting ourselves to different ways of life. To be tied and bound of necessity to one single way is not to live but to exist.

MONTAIGNE

Gotta get in my miles no matter what. . .

EVERY RUNNER

1981 AGAIN: CONSISTENCY IS DESIRABLE, and an ordinary runner (read: me) can be just as consistent as a superstar. Can't he? The daily bodily validation of one who runs is so clear, so basic. Why wouldn't anyone run every single day? But even at my most passionate, things did, some few days, seem to be in my way. Could that change?

Yes, I suppose the idea of an extended running streak had crossed my mind at one time or another, but I had made no New Year's resolution of it, always at bottom too superstitious to take on such a long chance against the icy aspect of early January, to say nothing of portly, post-holiday sloth.

Without having paid much attention to it, though, one day in the spring of 1981 I found myself coming up to the Boston Marathon with over one hundred straight days of running logged. In six years of moderately serious running, I'd never run that many in a row before. It must have been when I went out and (stiffly) ran the day after that as-usual-for-me frustrating Boston race that I decided to try to run every day for the rest of 1981, making it a solid year without missing a day.

It's easy to see, looking back, why I seized on this quirky task. It had to be some sort of warped penance, atonement for yet another Patriot's Day disappointment. (The Sisyphus Syndrome, I'd called it in a column back then, the annual Boston that ended up about five to ten minutes slower than my fall qualifier, thus dumping me back in the need-to-qualify pool. This year's version had been a 2:55.) Ideas born of frustration often have flaws, and this one proved to be no exception. Still, the idea was powerfully attractive, and nearly irresistible in its simplicity: just run a bit each day for the rest of the year.

OK, so I couldn't work out as hard or as fast or as much as Frank Shorter or Bill Rodgers. But by golly I *could* be as consistent! The words of Ron Daws in his fine book *The Self-Made Olympian* had the ring of truth: "When I'm full of running, I won't take a day off, for no other reason than I just want to see the mileage pile up in my log. I feel that if I let one day's running escape, the week will collapse." You're so right, Ron! Consistency was the key, the sure path to running success. My mileage, too, would pile up (Hadn't I just turned in my first-ever 300-mile month in March?) and I'd race better than ever.

So what if Ron Hill was fifteen years or more ahead of me in his ongoing running streak? All he'd have to do was miss *one little day* and he'd be the one playing catch-up! The clincher for this streaking business, as I saw it, was that it required absolutely no talent. Anyone could run as many days in a row as a world-class athlete, once any level of running would do. In fact, my chances in such a competition were better, since the risks of training and racing at elite levels would undoubtedly lay low a few of my rivals.

I had always respected the runners who got out every day. Though I generally do run most days, I seem to miss one every few weeks for one reason or another. In the last six weeks or so of most years, as well as from mid-April to around Memorial Day, I often miss days as I cut back for a planned rest period. Only when building up to a hard marathon, at most one in the spring and one in the fall, do I sometimes run through two or three months straight. My basic rule—one I admit I don't always follow—is to not miss any two days in a row.

All of which seemed sensible enough and in line with most training wisdom I'd encountered. Rest, after all, is an essential part of the stress/rest progressive training concept. But one person's rest is another person's hard run, and I was counting on two things in my proud springtime hopes. First, that I was very fit and thus strong enough to count as rest days easy runs of four or five miles. Second, that my main commitment was not to race hard or well or often, but only to run every day.

The problem with this impeccable logic was that I knew I *would* have to run hard at least a few times during the year. A total absence of racing, I knew, would render my running terminally boring.

I was accustomed to balancing running goals against life's other obligations, and was anticipating that as the difficult part of my streak-to-be. Only as the year un- folded did I begin to see how different kinds of running could conflict with one other. But in April it was easy to decide to take the plunge and run every day, come what might. Even if that meant foregoing, as I had the day after Boston, the virtuous (and helpfully recuperative) loafing indulged with honor after a hard race.

All spring I kept my commitment to myself, not wish- ing to stick my chin out too far. Those little voices inside me whispering their doubts had to be subdued. But at the end of June, as I met a couple of friends at the track, I was so filled with self-satisfaction at being halfway through my epic year that I couldn't help spilling out my plan to them. They were politely interested, but on the whole seemed to regard my scheme as having about the same value as running a marathon wearing swim fins instead of running shoes. Surely there were more important goals for which one could strive.

Whether or not they understood, I was ecstatic. Six months, half a year—and I had run every single day! I had put in more miles than in any previous six-month period. I was over the hump, and everything would go smoothly from now on.

Well, to be honest, there *was* one niggling dark cloud. A careful check of my log revealed that as of June 30, I had run 1,499 miles, rather than the 1500 I'd originally thought I'd done. 1,499 miles over six months does not mean the same as 1,500 miles, and anyone who thinks it does has not grasped the full import of the running log or the pleasures of compulsive record-keeping.

Most serious runners do keep track of their training mileage, and the more serious among these may in their zeal go to lengths of meticulousness that would do credit to a NASA scientist. At times I'm convinced that the truest runners have the souls of accountants. My log-book has plenty of space to record mileage for the day, to comment on the day's run, to note a weekly weight and distance checkpoint. Yet I manage to cover the margins with arcane scribblings as well, pace notations, symbols for particular courses, and an altogether ridiculous number of other details. I find, for example, wedged into a tiny space next to a daily box overflowing with split times from a 13-mile-plus race: "146lbsAM147for race after breakfast cereal banana tea 144 after race before bath but after 3 &1/2 beers & 2 hot dogs."

The heart of the logbook, though, is the once-blank inside front cover, on which I've created a grid of pure numbers, filled with a three-years-deep bank of comparative mileage totals, days run per month, records at year's beginning for some dozen distances with dates and paces given, and more. Lovingly entering my monthly totals as my streak built, I was a secret Seurat, creating dot by dot, stat by stat, a brilliant painting. Thus it was an ill omen indeed to discover that my ongoing yearly mileage total didn't agree exactly with the sum of the monthly totals listed. Finding a horrendous mistake in balancing my checkbook could not have been more disturbing!

As the summer months went by, more and more references to aching tendons and fatigue began to creep into the log, notes like the one after a longish run in August that ended "Seems it's been easier in the past." The effort involved in the streak was beginning to catch up with me.

In September I had to begin cranking up my level of training for my annual re-qualification for Boston. For the first time, I started a training phase without having taken it easy for at least a month beforehand. My body protested vehemently. The proverbial light bulb of wisdom lit up and I realized, in a new way, how hard it would be to keep my streak alive. As more costs became apparent in this task, I wondered if there might not be some costs I couldn't— or wouldn't—pay.

I persevered through the fall to a decent marathon, but only by limiting my concentration to that race alone. Then, with two months to go in the year, I turned my attention again to my Streak (now fully capitalized in my head), and when I did, it was with a lurch. Suddenly I had the feeling one gets in a race when one realizes there are more miles left than one can be sure of completing. Yes, I was eighty percent finished with the task, but that left twenty percent to go—more than two straight months of being a daily communicant at the shrine of running. I felt a jolt of doubt, recognizing the possibility of defeat.

What was I doing all this for, anyway? Who cared? With my streak in its eleventh month, I wasn't running fast anymore, wasn't putting in the record mileage I had early in the year (3,000 total? no way!), and I certainly wasn't healthier than ever before! Far from it. One of the ludicrous ways in which my body was taking me to task for not giving it a break was downright embarrassing: My face began to break out. Running my foolish way to fitness, I had middle-aged acne! Was this my reward? I wasn't running fast, nor far, nor even feeling good. I was just running.

In the end that was it: just running. Finally it dawned on me that merely by making the simple act of running itself the goal, streakers were demonstrating the purest of priorities. Somehow, through the alchemy of ordinary consistency, streakers were investing their runs with a special grandeur.

Still, I found myself wondering—when does a guy get a rest around here? I was prepared to admit I'd been wrong about this task being easy, but I had no one to confess to except myself. And how was I to stop—if I did—with just a month left to go? The year wasn't up. The task, however hard or easy, was still there. My will-power was in no better shape than the rest of my body, but I plodded on, the "rest" days—now mostly a weary three miles—just as draggy as the less and less frequent longer runs.

Shortly after a quite-long run in early December (see Chapter Five on a thirty-seven miler for my thirty-seventh birthday), I was handed a clear message: the Blood Bank turned me down because of low iron count. I was literally running myself into the ground. Two days after the Blood Bank bounced me, on December 13, it happened. I didn't run.

The ordeal was over, my streak gone. Two and a half weeks to go in 1981, and I hadn't been able to pull it off. How could I live with a defeat like that?

As it turned out, my compulsive record-keeping gave me a way out of my dilemma, though something of an oblique one. The night of my Blood Bank rejection, I was poking about despondently in my log, probably hoping to salvage some sense of accomplishment from the early days of the year when things looked rosier, when I made an unbelievable discovery: *I had come into the year, as it turned out, on a nineteen-day streak.* I hadn't been keeping close track back then, or perhaps, bedazzled by the end–of–year cornucopia of numbers to play with, had simply failed to carry the days over to the next year. By mid–April, when I was beginning to see the possibility of a year's streak, those nineteen days had been long forgotten.

Deliverance!

Lightning calculations showed me that by running just *one more day* I'd have 365 straight. Not a perfect calendar year, but enough of a victory for this tired runner. *A foolish consistency is the hobgoblin of little minds,* I thought to myself, and my grateful body congratulated me heartily on moving from the wisdom of Ron Daws to that of noted distance coach Ralph Waldo Emerson. Obviously Ron Hill and other serious streakers had nothing to fear from me. Still, I had benefitted from a glimpse at the size of the challenge they pose to themselves every day.

My last day's run was wonderful. Short, but wonderful. My log reads "rt. knee didn't feel too bad today." It also reads "Yay!" It fails entirely to truly capture the waves of satisfaction that rolled through me with every step, the immense feeling of achievement that filled me as I did my mile–and–a–half home–run trot around the cold gray streets of Somerville.

Tomorrow I could run or not run, but something would be different either way. I was a tad nervous about the long blank space ahead, and about the new necessity of having to decide whether or not to run each day. But my old inclination to devise a plan to fill every gap had burned out, and I ran happily through the raw winter morning, as blissed-out as if I'd just outkicked Alberto Salazar in front of the Prudential.

I had spent 364 days building up to this run, and it was resoundingly worth it. A foolish consistency, maybe, but a gratifying one as well.

CHAPTER FOUR

ODE TO CROSS COUNTRY

> . . . *over hill and dale out in the middle of nowhere.*
> *Spit freezing on your goddamn chin. Five hundred*
> *complete wild men in the mud, running up your heels*
> *with long spikes. Oh I love cross country all right. I also*
> *like being flayed alive with a rusty straight razor.*
>
> MILER QUENTIN CASSIDY
> IN *ONCE A RUNNER*, BY JOHN L. PARKER, JR.

STARTING LATE, WHEN I WAS fifty, I coached cross country at Concord–Carlisle High School for fourteen years. I
know that, though in general I ran less when coaching, I
learned more about running, and the ways running is like
life, through the experience. I was getting the daily running experience now of not just one person —me—but
that of about fifty people. Great stuff!

L et's hear it for obscurity! Among more commonly available sports, it's hard to find one to which less attention is paid than cross country. Track at least is known via folks watching the Olympics every few years, but cross country has no such visibility. Most high schools do in fact have a cross country program of sorts—and why not, given that equipment costs are low and it doesn't take up space "real" sports are using (gyms, playing fields). But if you ask, most students or teachers at any school would have to admit they'd never seen a cross country meet, and probably would further admit they weren't sure when or where such meets happen. And when was the last time you settled down in front of the TV, cracked open a cold one to go with the chips and dip, and watched a cross country meet?

I thought so. Neither have I.

Yet I'd like to. Cross country is exactly as wonderful as it is obscure, perhaps the ideal blend of team and individual sport, of simplicity and complexity, of the accessible and the arcane. I would not have gushed so eloquently about the sport's virtues after my initial cross country race experience, though.

It was back in the late 1980's, and I'd been drafted by my club, Cambridge Sports Union, to fill out a team for a cross country event at Boston's Franklin Park—their masters B team, I believe it was. I hadn't been doing much racing at all, but must have showed up and hung near a six-minute pace for a Fresh Pond two-and-a-half miler on a Saturday when some fellow CSU-ers were thinking about the upcoming event, and must have said OK when asked if I was interested in helping out. I'm sure I was flattered to be asked to run with a team, since that was a rarity, and, by then a veteran road racer, didn't bother to reveal my ignorance about cross country versus road racing. I didn't know, in fact, how much I didn't know.

My memory of that first true cross country race is painful. The race took place on what is now considered the regular Franklin Park course, though stretched to eight K (five miles) rather than the five K (just over three miles) I'm now used to seeing run in the high school racing world. A second loop of what's called at Franklin "the Wilderness," and a second ramble over "Bear Cage Hill" made up the extra, as I recall. The oddest thing to road-racer Tom was that they had actually put hay bales on the course for the racers to jump over in several places. Huh? Hay bales? Hadn't seen anything like that in my decade-plus of road racing! Now, it was okay to simply run around the bales if you wanted to, but of course then you were adding distance which, however small, is never a good competitive strategy.

What I learned that day was that eight kilometers of cross country was way harder, and therefore seemed way longer, than the same distance in a road race. The soft turf seemed to suck energy from my every stride; the hills seemed much more daunting than any road hills. The bales, which appeared only during the second loop, were simply impossible; I veered around them, muttering.

I also learned that the crowd who came to participate in any cross country event was one tough bunch. In the average road race, then as now, a significant number of folks are generally trying out racing for the first time, or just out for a sociable ramble. Any reasonably fit road racer will therefore finish in front of a large percentage of the field in most road races. Even in my not-in-great-shape forties this was the case for me—heck, anything under eight-minute mile pace would put one in the top third of most road races.

But in this cross country world I was a baby, a rookie, a weakling. There I was, busting my butt in this awful cross country thing, working as hard as I could to try to do right by my teammates—and the field drew inexorably farther from me. By the last mile the idea that I was actually competing had been rendered ridiculous. If I wasn't dead last, I might as well have been. I had clearly stepped into a new turf, one peopled by grizzled woods creatures who understood this stuff in ways I did not.

I didn't know it then, for example, but I'm sure in retrospect that most of the competitors that day were wearing spikes. I had never touched, much less worn, spiked racing shoes. I'm pretty sure I was unaware of their existence as basic tools for racing cross country. Since pretty much all my running experience had been on pavement, spikes sticking out of the bottoms of my feet was an imaginative leap I was simply incapable of making. And the nice even pacing that worked well on roads needed adjustments, ones I didn't know how to make in the ups and downs of cross country.

I dimly recall painfully slogging to the finish line, then meandering around commiserating with a few other beat-up tail-enders. I had no idea about how the race had gone for my team, and what, if any, role I'd played in their scoring, or even how that scoring worked. And I was too miserable to care. And that remains my last real experience as a cross country competitor. Why, then, do I love this sport so deeply?

Unlikely as it might seem, I came to love cross country by coaching it.

I've been a lucky fellow in many ways, and one stroke of luck was that in the early 1990s a CSU running buddy of mine, Maureen, who lived in Concord, became the coach of the girls cross country team at the high school there, where I taught. I'd been interested in the team—I was a runner, after all—but only from afar, so to speak, in my first decade at the school, since babies at home and commuting out to Concord from Dorchester daily meant that hanging around even to watch athletic events was somewhat problematic, and regularly spending long afternoons at the school with a team would have been impossible.

But when we moved to town and the kids were older things loosened up. The first fall we lived in Concord I got to a couple of meets and went out to practices a couple of times, still clueless about what a coach might actually do, and when Maureen decided to step down from the coaching position after that season, I thought this might be a nice new experience for me, and put in my bid to take over. The Athletic Director kindly overlooked my complete lack of coaching experience and hired me on the basis that first, I was a faculty member in good standing, and second, I had known organizational skills. (This shown by my having taken over the faculty football pool from this same AD with successful results.) That I'd been a runner for twenty years and had multiple sub-2:50 marathons under my belt and had published some stuff in running magazines seemed to show that I must know *something* about how to train and run. So the deal was done, and I became a coach.

Fifteen years later, I know now how ridiculously little I knew then.

My central assumption was that the girls on the team, since they were runners, were something like myself, and that I could apply what I knew about training and racing in my own experience to them. Wrong. There were around fifteen girls on the team that first year, and that meant, I soon learned, that there were fifteen different reasons for being there, fifteen different personalities, fifteen different approaches and none of them was much like my own. And that remains the case now—even more so, in fact, with fifty to sixty girls regularly on the team.

I started off with a couple of pretty good years, actually, as the girls recorded winning seasons (5-3) in (what I came to learn later was) a pretty tough league. We ran to a 4-4 record my third year. My approach was a loose one: If you want to succeed, you will do the necessary work. Since the girls knew this, it seemed OK to outline for them what they ought to be doing on Saturdays and Sundays, and not to run practices on the weekends. Oh, once in a while there would be a Saturday invitational meet we'd go to, but essentially their team commitment was a five-day one.

My fourth season was memorably bad. I'd had a couple of bright young sophomore runners the year before, but they decided together that they needed to be focused on their studies as juniors, and didn't come out for the team. The brightest star, who'd set a freshman record on our course the previous year, had a season-ending injury in the first meet. My strongest runner all year was a senior soccer convert who alternated between showing great promise and spraining and re-spraining an ankle. The better runner of my two co-captains moved away the summer before our season. What could go wrong, did go wrong. We failed to win a meet all year, finishing a perfect 0-8.

Well, as I said to the assembled troops at our post-season banquet, you're supposed to learn more from defeats than from victories, and we should celebrate the wonderful learning experience we'd created. And in fact, in a steady progression over the next few years we became one of the elite teams in the state, and enjoyed that status as I turned in my clipboard and stopped coaching after fourteen years last season. How did a 0-8 team become, two years later, a competitor, and then a fixture, at the state meet?

I remember the first state meet I ever went to, at the end of my third year, in 1997. My senior all-star, who'd been carrying the team along on her shoulders for all my three coaching years, had qualified as an individual runner to compete at states by finishing among the top seven runners not on a qualifying (top five) team at the regional class meet. At the state meet, held that year at Franklin Park, it snowed! Dory and I had to scrounge around to try to find some longer spikes for her racing shoes, and I still think her just-average-for-her perfor- mance there could've been better had I been readier as a coach to help her meet the conditions.

But what did I know about spikes? Nothing, given that I had never worn them in my own road racing exper- ience, however considerable. Dory may have been the only athlete on the team that year who even wore spikes. These days, on my teams of fifty or sixty girls, about half will have spikes, and I certainly make a point of pitch- ing their virtues to the team early and often. What, back then, did I know about post-season racing at all?

Our experience that snowy Saturday taught me some- thing about preparedness and New England's propensity for crappy post-season meet weather and conditions. Beyond that, it began my education in the wider context of late season Big Meet-ism. At that time, I still didn't even know how the teams that got to the state race earned their spots, technically, and the following year (the disas- trous winless one mentioned earlier) we were so awful, and so beat up by the end of our regular season, that the team—and it was a team decision—simply didn't go to the EMass qualifying meet at all. Why bother? A year later, although we still lost more than we won, we'd done a complete about-face, improved to a mid-pack showing at our league meet, and watched girls on a qualifying team dancing after the class meet race, saying to ourselves "Next year that's us."

And it was—two years after going winless, we went 6-2 and qualified for the state meet by running fourth at the regional class meet. The following year we won the class meet, and the expectations since then have always been, from the start of the year, to get to the state meet. It was the awareness of the goal that engendered the ability to achieve the goal.

When you have a goal, you know you have to find a path towards it somehow, and the main characteristic of that path for us was knowing we had to practice more and work harder. A shift to six-day practice weeks and a harder workload somehow translated to more girls wanting to run on the team. And more girls, working harder, meant more success, which attracted still more girls.

A frame of reference was established, so the girls actually knew what success was, what their race times meant on our course, and how, specifically, to attack our course. Maureen and her runner-husband, Jake, had put the course together using trails in the woods behind the school mixed with some loops of the school's complex of athletic fields. When I started coaching, I had no records of what had been done in past years. There hadn't been that many, in fact, as Maureen only was there for a few years, and prior to her time the girls had run the same course as the guys did, which included some terrific woodsy trails in a town forest but required (yikes!) crossing a main road mid-race. Her design brought the whole race onto our campus, a big safety plus. And a couple of years after I started coaching the girls, the guys' team moved to the same course.

It was one of the shorter courses in our league then, 2.67 miles, and all natural surfaces. The fastest guys (but not many) could break 14:00 on it, the fastest girls (again very few) could beat 17:00. There was just one hill—a serious one, though not that long—in the first mile, but the second, wooded mile was brutal, with three or four tough climbs, plus a section I liked to call the "roller coaster," featuring a series of short but sharp ups and downs. When you gratefully thundered down a hill and out of the woods, you had to turn back into them thirty meters later to close the second mile with the steepest climb of the course. Forget even pacing. The question was never would you slow down for the second mile, but always just "how much?" Then the last two-thirds of a mile were downhill, a hairpin turn, and a final flat lap (c.700 meters) of the lower athletic fields. The top girls could survive the course well enough to take advantage of that closing piece and run below four minutes for their final two-thirds of a mile.

I began to keep course records over the years for all of our girls in the form of an honor roll of sub-20:00 runners, and all girls from competing schools in our league who broke 19:00. Girls who broke 18:00 were all-league caliber, and girls capable of beating 17:00 were monster all-Scholastic types. Only three girls from my school had cracked that 17-minute barrier, plus seven others from the league's then-eight schools, when the course had to be re-configured in 2007. That's ten girls total, over about fifteen years. This list, keeping track of performances, was a major incentive-builder. The girls also knew the Franklin Park EMass course better and better, and I kept lists of all sub-22:00 times there to supplement our home course lists.

As we became more aware of the larger context of weekend invitational meets and post-season events, it became clear that we were fortunate to be in a very strong league. You get better when you run against top teams, and we had lots of good ones to compete against. The 2009 State Meet, for example, saw four girls' teams from our league finish in the top nine teams of Division One. There are around one hundred teams statewide in that division—four of the top nine from one league!

I had been a decent middle-aged road racer because I could find the time to build a lot of running into my life, averaging around eight miles per day, a bit more during marathon build-ups, for years. And the way I did that was to squeeze in running in many barely-available places. I'd commute by running into work. I'd run during lunches. I'd get up early to get in a training run before a busy workday. As a teacher, I'd make use of a free period. But all of this meant that the focus was on getting the RUN part in, and that long warm-ups, cool-downs, and stretching periods weren't possible. That was fine with me, and I happened to get away with that approach most of the time, running without major injuries for long periods.

But that was exactly wrong for my team of high school girls (and would have been for guys, too). They need to warm up properly, cool down effectively, and stretch religiously, or their vulnerable bodies (however invulnerable they feel themselves to be) will suffer. A problem here is that most of the girls would agree with me that all that good stretching stuff is also pretty boring. My early focus was on running and running and more running, but now I know I have to get the team to buy into the other stuff, or we'll have trouble staying competitive. Gotta stretch. Gotta do the core srength-building exercise circuits. The bottom line: the athletes have to feel good about doing the healthy stretching and other protective warm–up and cool-down routines, and the only way to get them to do that is to turn a half-hour post-run stretching session into a pleasurable experience hanging with their buddies. The team members must like each other, must enjoy all their time together, must think practice a fun place to be. So: teach the routines, and also build the team bonds well. And that exemplifies the double approach needed: be present and instructive, but also be able to get out of the way and let the team enjoy each other. I always enjoyed running with the girls, but discovered as the years went by that the less I ran with them, the better they raced.

Coaching was certainly one of the things I liked best during my time at the school. The palpable results were enormously gratifying, and my personal satisfaction was always exponentially enlarged as it multiplied and rippled through the consciousnesses of fifty or so girls having their own experiences of success at all different levels. Helping students towards better writing is wonderful, but proof of progress is elusive and hard to judge. When your team takes the top five spots in a cross country meet, though, its demonstration of excellence is clear to all. When a girl first breaks twenty minutes for five kilometers, it's marvelously measurable. And the resonating of all the success stories is great: kids love being on a good team, and enjoy their teammates' successes as much as their own.

An important routine during the season was always the Thursday team meeting the day after a Wednesday meet. I could give out my weekly race write-ups and debrief the team on plusses and problems shown in their racing, as well as setting the tone and training structure for the week ahead. More important, the girls themselves chipped in with comments on their experiences, praising each other and generally sharing the joy. "It was so helpful to run with Jess," one would say, or "When we came out of the woods and saw all the freshmen cheering it was so awesome," and so on. Of course, this plays better following a win, but we also made good use of its therapeutic qualities after our (infrequent) losses. The principle of accepting and celebrating the ordinary has played a central role in my coaching, and it is a strategy that brings wins.

When giving out my own old road-race t-shirts as recognitions of special performances in races at our next-day team meetings, I gave out shirts to course record breakers and winners, but I gave out as many to girls who were in the middle of the pack, or even near the end of it. Their experiences had to be honored as well.

For the first few years I coached, among other post-season banquet highlights was always giving out our Most Valuable Runner award. But as the years went by, other awards proliferated: Most Improved, Best Teammate, Rookie of the Year, then (teams ever-enlarging) Upperclass Rookie of the Year and Freshperson Rookie of the Year. Each year some girls were given Iron Horse awards for participating in every single race—and here the winners were as likely to be pokey puppies as all-stars, only consistency mattered. The more things we found to celebrate on the team, the better the team got.

In the awards expansion, I also wanted to try to build a sense of history and continuity, so I re-named the Most Valuable Runner award, calling it the Dory Folk award to connect it to my first all-star. Discussing the virtues a particular girl had brought to our team made the award mean more. And the same year I re-named that award I created a second major award called the Becky Broadwin award. Becky had been a model cross country team girl: she'd improved from a very ordinary freshperson season enough to earn a spot as our sixth or seventh girl as a sophomore, a year when we won our Eastern Massachusetts regional meet. We had four league all-stars that year, but Becky was not one of them. She never made the league all-star team, in fact, though she continued to improve

each year and was a captain her senior year. By her senior
year, in fact, the team itself was so much stronger that,
despite her own continued improvement, Becky didn't
make our top seven to run at the state meet. But it was
the improvement of our mid-level runners, like Becky,
that made the team as a whole so much stronger. The new
award recognized girls who brought the qualities Becky
brought to the team: dedication, determination, upbeat
spirits, consistency, a team ethic. Now I'm proud that the
only two award plaques in our school's crowded athlet-
ics trophy display case named for students are from cross
country, and that one of them celebrates the extraordinary potential of the ordinary runner.

The sources of strength for my cross country teams
came from its acceptance of weakness. To begin with, we
were one of the few no-cuts teams at the school. If you
came out, you were on the team, period. The bigger we
got, the better we got, and of course that makes sense:
isn't it likely that there will be a few more fast runners in
a big crowd than in a small one? But aside from those few
faster ones, ALL the runners improve more reliably, in
my view, on a bigger team.

What's great for the girls is the feeling of arriving at
another school for a meet and having the other team
regard them with awe, with respect. *Wow, there are so
many of them! Wow, they look as though they're having fun!
Oooh, I love how they seem to be communicating in their pre-
race circle!* And it's true that there's an intimidation factor
here, too. When your little band of fifteen or twenty

girls sees sixty girls tumbling off a bus you have to wonder just a little.

Coaching can teach kids how to be able to train or race better, but also teaches them how to appreciate building towards something, how to create and then celebrate growth and progress. As always, it comes back to paying attention: I'm trying to teach the girls to pay attention to their training, to their success, to that of their teammates.... because attention paid will always bring a reward. And there's a world of stuff to pay attention to here, if you know where to look.

That said, looking at a cross country race, especially the first time or so, isn't that great, really, for most people. You see flashes, and in those flashes you see crowds of runners, most of whom are indistinguishable from one another, thundering past in big lumps. There can be exciting duels at any point over the race, most clearly seen in closing-stretch battles between desperate kickers running on guts and fumes. But that's one tiny part of a big race—if that's what made one come to see cross country races, it'd be fine to show up for about one minute and just watch that.

But say you have a kid on a team—then your interest goes up. You have an individual to focus on and a team to root for. Then say you watch not just one race, but follow the team through several races, and begin to know a few of the other runners by sight, to anticipate where they'll be in the order of the race, in relation to your kid, then in the larger order of the race. And you also begin to get a sense of the team's home course, where the big breaks in the race come—how the group tends to look when they run into the second (woodsy, hilly) mile and the significance of the change on the order of things when they come out of those woods again with less than a mile to go. Your watching begins to be of a qualitatively different order. Now coach a team for ten or fifteen years, participate in structuring the course, and know what this particular race means to each of your team's participants, who's having a breakthrough day, who's struggling. Can you feel it yet? In this scenario you've come to the race with a whole team-load of expectations and hopes and plans—and they all are playing out simultaneously in front of you. What a rush! That's what coaching is about, and cross country allows it to be encapsulated in about twenty non-stop minutes of excitement. Stretch four races, a varsity and a JV race for each gender, over a couple of fall-afternoon hours, and watching cross country ranks right up there with any sports spectating I know.

What could be better? A team sport where all players perform the same act at the same time (Are there other sports where that happens? Think about it...), yet each person has his or her own special experience, and has his or her performance measured with exact ruthlessness. As I claimed above, it's the perfect blend of team and individual sport.

How is this so? Look at the way it's scored: When two teams run against each other, only their top seven runners are officially in the scoring, and only the scores of the top five count towards the team total. More than seven may participate at times—our league has guidelines of twelve runners in a varsity race and allows unlimited runners in JV races—but for scoring purposes, only seven runners count. So if two teams race, there are fourteen official result places available, and the scoring is straightforward: first-place runner gets one point, second place two, third three, and so on down to fourteenth place. Low score wins. The best score you can get, clearly, therefore, is a fifteen—1-2-3-4-5. The fun stuff starts with the concept of displacement. Displacement happens when one team's sixth or seventh runner comes in ahead of any of the opponent's top five. That means that the opponent's fifth scoring runner will get pushed down past the top ten, taking an eleven or twelve score that's very damaging. Pretty simple, though, right? Add 'em up and low total for your top five wins.

Here's an example:

A few years ago, first meet of the season, first home meet for us at Concord-Carlisle. Excitement all around— it's a three-way meet between Concord-Carlisle and our two biggest league rivals, Newton South and Lincoln-Sudbury. Those are two super programs, always strong: as I write this, they've been the 1-2 teams at the Massachusetts state meet for several years running, and as recently as 2008 placed sixth and twelfth at the Nike Nationals super season-closing team race of the top qualifying twenty or so teams in the country! Meanwhile Concord-Carlisle were opening that year as defending EMass champions, and even with their major returning all-star sitting the meet out with an injury, thought they could compete.

The event matched its pre-meet hype fully. A gorgeous afternoon saw a pack of leaders press a strong pace. Three leaders, one from each school, were bunched at one mile, with another mixed pack of a half-dozen girls in close pursuit, and a hard-working train chugging not far behind them. Coming out of the woods two girls led, and after they struggled up to the two-mile mark, C-C's other returning league all-star, Liz Coogan, had broken away. She ran a super race to win by eleven seconds in a 17:08 time that was then seventh best all-time for the hilly 2.67 mile course.

Nice start for team CCXC , but the other two schools then sent the next six finishers across the line, each thus with three in before our second. Team frustration follows Liz's elation. But wait! Now the next three girls—hooray—are from the home team. Hope leaps forth anew! And then it's a tossed salad of finishers in a bunch and spectators are doing internal math as fast as they can but no one knows how it came out as the runners gasp and hug and stretch and drift off for cool-downs, catch-ups, and commiserations, and coaches crouch around clipboards squinting at results.

OK, time for some really fun math. Here's the individual finish order for scoring:

1. Concord-Carlisle
2. Lincoln-Sudbury
3. Newton South
4. Newton South
5. Lincoln-Sudbury
6. Lincoln-Sudbury

7. Newton South
8. Concord–Carlisle
9. Concord– Carlisle
10. Concord–Carlisle
11. Lincoln–Sudbury
12. Newton South
13. Concord–Carlisle
14. Newton South
15. Concord–Carlisle
16. Lincoln–Sudbury

And another dozen or so finishers, since schools can run up to twelve varsity. Can you juggle these numbers and name a winner?

First, you have to understand that when three schools run in a race this way, it's scored as two simultaneously-happening two-team meets, so three sets of results are generated, each using just two of the schools, in this case for example, Concord-Carlisle versus Newton South, Concord-Carlisle versus Lincoln-Sudbury, and Newton South versus Lincoln-Sudbury. Got that? Here's how it turned out.

Concord-Carlisle lost to South that day by a point, South's 2-3-4-8-10 = 27 nosing out C-C's 1-5-6-7-9 = 28. Meanwhile, L-S edged South, 1-4-5-7-10 = 27 to 2-3-6-8-9 = 28. But—and here's what makes it amazing— Concord-Carlisle beat L-S, tying their score and then winning because the sixth C-C runner beat L-S's sixth, the tie-break factor in a deadlocked race. And displacement was the key, as C-C's sixth girl had actually beaten L-S's fifth finisher too, forcing the tie AND winning the tie-break as well. C-C were 1-5-6-7-9 (and 10) = 28 (exactly, note, their score versus South) while L-S, taking that big 11 for their fifth, went 2-3-4-8-11 = 28, then lost on the tie-break. All three schools started the season even at a win and a loss, 1-1, a blah-sounding record after an epic race. You can bet rival coaches checking out those scores in the morning paper were scratching their heads!

Note the profusion of heroines: Liz's super victory, but also the three-girl 8-9-10 Concord-Carlisle pack. And really, the event-changer was Concord-Carlisle's sixth finisher, Kristin Hurlbut, at fifteenth-place overall. In effect she'd emerged as the winner of a race-within-a-race between the second five girls of all three teams. Every girl out there was involved somehow—a great demonstration of the team nature of this sport.

It's a bit different in the big multi-school meets. With squads strictly limited to seven racers, your team score is simply the total of your top five runners' places. Whereas the worst number your team can have added to its score in a dual meet is a twelve—their fifth scoring place after the other team's allowable seven recognized runners—in a field of thirty or forty schools and hundreds of racers, your fifth-place scorer might take an ugly enough individual number, say, 198, to offset two, three, or even four strong performances from the rest of your team. Meanwhile putting five girls between twenty-fifth and thirty-fifth will leave you with a team total under 150, and possibly competitive for team honors. Your fourth and fifth runners thus become even more important as the meets get bigger, and your sixth and seventh are crucial, both for insurance against a bad race or injury and as pushers-down of rival schools' mid-pack numbers. Superstars help, but depth wins.

Coaching involves evaluation, and making constantly-shifting judgments about whether a girl's improving or slipping back, working up to her potential or not. But though one thinks in this judgmental way all the time, one doesn't issue real report cards. I'm an easy grader as far as how I'd rate girls on my team, on their always-invisible reports.

Almost all would get A's, with a smattering of B's. The efforts and the joys of the girls are too apparent not to honor. After all, this is a "course" taken only by those who have elected to do so, and of the many elements that go into being on a team, most do not require special athletic skill. It makes clear sense that this self-selected class should do well. If I see a girl is serious enough about her racing to want an evaluative breakdown of her 20:37 5K performance, I can talk about taking a more aggressive approach at the start, or sticking more closely to another runner early in the race, or a way to relax through a key mid-race stretch .... but I can't tell a mud-soaked sophomore who's run worse than her PR in a monsoon that she just got a C+. Also, in this "course" the homework all gets done right in class because the class/practice, for the most part, consists of exactly that: doing the homework. Wow, an open-to-all, elective honors class where everyone does well and doesn't bring home homework when class ends. That this class meets six days a week for from two-plus hours to four or more on meet days does give it an edge over, let's say, five English classes of fifty-five minutes each, and maybe an hour a day of homework for five or six days. Eleven hours for English (or math, or science) versus seventeen or more for the sport.

Hmmm. . . .

Whatever the time commitment amounts to, what should be going on is training the girls to a habit of self-examination and conscious seeking of improvement. Of course, that's just what should have been be going on in my English classroom, as well. And though I'm quite sure it did get done there, too, I'm willing to admit that there may have been a higher percentage of it on my cross country teams.

And rarely, even in the best of my classes, did a student taking, say, American Lit Survey need to put forth the intense effort my cross country girls did so heroically day in and day out. For most of the last few years I coached, the school's principal was a particular fan of our teams (boys' as well as girls'). He'd been a runner himself, a very good one in fact, the answer to the trivia question "Who holds the indoor mile record at the Boston Garden?" (It will, now that there is no more Boston Garden, forever be Art Dulong's 4:01 from forty years ago.) Before coming to Concord-Carlisle, Art had taught for years next door at Lexington High, where he'd also put together a hall-of-fame coaching career in track and cross country.

In other words, this fellow knew a lot more than I did about serious competitive running and coaching, and yet Art never ever advised or even offered suggestions, content to enjoy our success when he could and mostly from afar. I tried to draw him out, in fact, on a number of occasions, but only once did he offer me his wisdom on cross country. This was to tell me how much he respected all the runners because of how incredibly *hard* the sport was. It took so long, Art said, and gave you so many opportunities to simply quit. Whatever you did on the track, however painful it was, whether a sprint or a mile, was going to end in seconds or, at most, minutes. Cross country instead has one steadily pushing for fifteen or twenty or more minutes, often where there are no spectators. In our huge JV races, where slower girls might take up to half an hour for 5K, I had to give them credit for heroically sticking to the task.

I'm not coaching now—in fact, I'm not even really running any more. Sustained running has been off my agenda of possibilities since the removal of my cancerous lung, and my long-planned retirement from teaching has included a retirement from coaching.

I still love going to races, but my major link to cross country today is that I find myself walking on routes we used for cross country workouts. When I walk around Walden Pond, of course I think about ancient soul-mate Henry's time there in his little shack, and chuckle ironically to see the many signs urging pedestrians to Stay on the Paths to Prevent Erosion. How anti-Thoreauvian!

But I also think of the joy I've felt standing on the main beach end and watching fifty girls stretched out in single file trotting along the path into the woods on the far side during a practice. It is sheer glee imagining Thoreau, maybe that day joined by a visiting Margaret Fuller, watching the line of galloping girls—such wonderment, such thoughts those stern critics each would have! What I'd give to read about such a vision in Thoreau's journal! When I ramble through the woodsy trails around what's been called Mount Misery since before Thoreau's time, I think of Henry and his buddy Ellery Channing picnicking there, but also think about the Doom Loops workout the team has up and down the "kettle trails" in those woods once or twice a season.

Clambering up a hill on the Battle Road trail walk these days, I recognize it as a turnaround spot on a nine-mile run route I'd made a regular for the top girls. When I'm on the observation tower at Great Meadows National Wildlife Refuge I may be scanning with the scope to search for a couple of visiting swans, but I also remember the pleasure of scoping a group of cross country heads bobbing along at a good clip behind a screen of reeds along the far side of the causeway loop, pigtails across the marshes.

In a way, this sort of thing is problematic today, since such thoughts are reminders that I am very clearly NOT running those trails, but rather walking them, and with no team to watch, either. Do I really need reminders of what I loved but no longer do, even can't do? Of course not, but it's still good to be there. I'll let the ghosts add flavor to the present, but I won't let them overwhelm it. The focus must be on what I'm doing, not what I'm not doing. My daily run has simply become my daily walk. My quiet personal time of losing myself in a routine of physical activity is still my quiet personal time. It's just taking longer and I'm not sweating.

Cross country—where different courses and different conditions make every race unique, and where the struggling runner has ample time to dwell on distress signals and to despair, but has to go on anyway. Where every athlete in the race is doing the same thing, starting and finishing in the same place, but where each runner is having his or her own personal, singular experience of the event unfolding. Sound familiar? Isn't this life? I'm not running any more, no, but I still, and thankfully, seem to be in some fashion doing cross country.

CHAPTER FIVE

THE THIRTY-SEVEN MILE UNMARKED INVISIBLE ACID TEST

There is no exercise that is either feebler or more strenuous, according to the nature of the mind concerned, than that of conversing with one's own thoughts.

MONTAIGNE

I'D HEARD FROM MY FATHER about my old Riverside, Connecticut, neighbor Jim Fixx doing something similar long before he was a famous running-book author, and the idea of commemorating a birthday by running that birthday's number of miles had been in my mind for a long time. I recommend the experience, especially to my younger readers!

69

A sunny day in early December, 1981. I could see Boston's glossy skyscrapers, the Prudential Center and the John Hancock Building, in the distance as I trotted through the considerably less shiny neighborhoods of Somerville across the river. It was about noon of a wonderfully unseasonable winter running day, temperatures climbing through the forties, and I mentally checked off details as I ran.

Let's see. I'd just made a stop to change into fresh running clothes, and my daypack held another dry jersey and a t-shirt if I needed them. Had I remembered to bring those socks I wanted to exchange in Harvard Square? Yep. I had some money in the pocket of my all-weather running suit. Legs felt pretty loose. My stomach—those just-gulped cookies and that quick swig of milk sloshing around in it—seemed okay.

The fourteen-plus mile suburban loop out to Lexington and back was behind me now. Only a little over 22 to go, and still reasonably close to schedule. My thirty-seven mile run on my thirty-seventh birthday was progressing satisfactorily. The only detail that remained slightly fuzzy as I set out, the only question to which I couldn't fire back a fast answer, was surely the most interesting one: Why was I doing this?

It seemed like a good idea at the time would have been as valid an answer as any, I suppose. I'd considered the run more carefully than that, however, and had reasons enough, or at least enough to satisfy me. In the first place, thirty-seven miles on my thirty-seventh birthday was a project that had the kind of quirky numerical logic to which a great many runners, including myself, are addicted. A large part of running's charm, after all, is that it generates such a wealth of precise numbers, numbers we can squirrel away in our logs as fastests, farthests, and other personal treasures.

Also, I was strongly drawn to the novelty of the experience. I'd never run farther than the marathon distance, which meant that this journey would take me through more than ten miles of unexplored territory. I can't believe there are many runners who haven't wondered what would happen if they got out there five, ten, or more miles beyond their previous longest run. I hadn't extended my horizons so precipitously since my first marathon, years earlier.

Finally, beyond this desire to take a cautious dip into the ultra-running waters, I had decided that this run was a perfect birthday present to myself. And a fine extravagant one it was, too: a gift of the day, set aside for only this run of ridiculous and glorious length.

So I had plenty of good reasons to be out there ambling all over town—or towns, more properly: Somerville, Arlington, Lexington, Cambridge, Boston. I started out at about a 7:45 pace, more than half a minute per mile slower than I usually trained, and every three or four miles I'd walk for about five minutes. The plan was to take it easy throughout, and to be finished after roughly six hours (though I confess I harbored the secret hope that I could do it in closer to five).

I was in decent shape for such an expedition. A month earlier I'd run my fastest marathon in a little under 2:45. Aside from a low-key five-mile race two weeks after that, I'd not done any hard running work since, but I'd kept plugging along at 55 to 60 miles a week. I felt quite confident (innocent that I was!) about going the full distance, even though I couldn't really imagine what those last five or ten miles would feel like.

For the morning loop, the first stage of the run, I'd headed out to Lexington, a familiar route. About halfway there I'd walked for a bit—though I certainly hadn't yet felt any need for a break—and then had walked again when I got to the center of Lexington itself. Buying a giant cookie and some juice (I'd not wanted to carry anything heavier than a few dollar bills on this first stage) stretched this break to nearly ten minutes as I strolled around Battle Green and the famous Minuteman statue.

Heading homeward out of town I'd passed an old-fashioned iron direction post on a little circle at a place where the road split. Reading its mileages— Concord 7, Stoneham 8, Lowell 16, Boston 12—and knowing I was going to run farther than any of those towns had given me a fine feeling of freedom. After another short walk about halfway back, I'd arrived back at my house in Somerville feeling pretty fresh. A short change-and-eat break and then I shoved off again, doing my mental checklist.

I felt good. And yet there was an odd note below the surface somewhere, a rankling feeling of unfulfilled expectation. Aside from that brief flash at the signpost, these two-plus hours on the move hadn't quite achieved the specialness I'd hoped for. The epic quality of the run hadn't made itself felt, and I was impatient, looking for something, well . . . *new*.

My first break on this second stage of the run came just two miles later, in Harvard Square. It turned out to last slightly longer than expected, as exchanging my splendid but overlarge birthday gift socks became moderately complex. Just entering the store was a comedown. It seemed tiny and dark after a morning spent in the sunny expanses of my journey. Then there was the clerk, a tall, weedy fellow engaged, when I arrived, in what seemed to me particularly trivial chatter with some lingering customers.

Dealing with people after two and a half hours on the road, in the middle of a long run, is not unlike dealing with people right after you've become a parent. You're extremely alert, even speedy. You expect everyone to recognize instinctively a special quality about you and to treat you with great consideration. Anything less grates; you get grumpy. Doesn't this fellow *know* I have twenty miles still to run? Can't he devote a little attention to someone engaged in so noble a project?

When the clerk did, finally, turn to me, prompt answers to my questions seemed beyond him. I mean, come *on!* How hard could it be for him to come up with a smaller pair of those snappy brown argyles for a terrific guy like me, a hero of the road?

Leaving, I grumped my way over to the river and down to M.I.T., where I met my one pre-arranged mid-run connection of the day. I'd told my friend Stephen that I'd be there around 12:30, figuring that gave me ample margin for error, but my schedule, loose though it was, was already breaking down, and I got there closer to one o'clock. The last five miles, with breaks, had taken about fifty minutes. Stephen handed me some apple juice, and after walking with him for a few minutes I pushed off again. Over the bridge to the Boston side and back upriver.

I wasn't exactly *tired* at that point, but a growing realization began to take hold. I'd been on this run for three and a half hours and still had hours to go. The sheer amount of time on my feet was going to become a critical factor. I remembered Bill Rodgers's remarks about the toughness of four-hour marathoners, how he respected their ability to keep on their feet and hard at it for so long, something he never had to do.

Although I hadn't gone into a new *distance* range yet, I was on the edge of running for a longer *time* than ever before. And with well over two hours still ahead, I was getting my first glimpse of the size of the task I'd taken on. I began to see that one element in the new equation I was creating as I ran was a certain undercurrent, not altogether undesirable, of fear.

I really needed the water-and-stretching stop at the Harvard boathouse after crossing the river again at about twenty-three miles, and was glad to take another break a few miles later as I neared Fresh Pond Reservoir in Cambridge. Here I made a side trip to a little store where I picked up my last provisions. I ate as I walked, and finished the carob-raisin-nut snack and apple juice as I arrived at the Pond.

I had by now almost covered the marathon distance, about four and one quarter hours after starting out. I was entering what I'd envisioned as the third and last stage of my trip. I was very tired now, but here I would find my reward, here each mile would surely be special. Five laps of the two-and-a-quarter mile main course around the reservoir, with a short walk to begin each lap, would take me to the magic thirty-seven mark.

Runners generally have some route on which they feel most comfortable, some course they consider their running "home." Fresh Pond was certainly mine, and arriving there gave this fading novice ultrarunner a much-needed psychological lift. Here I was also able to check my progress against mile markers, and was pleasantly surprised to find that I was still moving along—when running—at not too far above an eight-minute pace. I was tight, I was slowing, but I was going to make it.

Probably.

I hadn't doubted that when I began, but back there nearly thirty miles and four and a half hours ago the miles were abstract, and each one was now assuming laborious reality.

I had read Tom Osler's excellent training books, and had also virtually memorized James Shapiro's wonderful

reports from the ultra front. Osler made his point clearly:
If one was in shape to run a 2:45 marathon, one could
quite conceivably (with a careful approach) break seven
hours in a fifty-mile race. One could, given a decent
running background, double one's longest run by mixing
walking with running and by drinking lots of fluids,
preferably sugary ones. My thirty-seven mile run had
thus seemed eminently possible, even something of a lark,
and I'd decided the key was to approach it with a light-
hearted attitude, with no rigidly-set goal for the time it
would take.

This enlightened view, sensible as it was, didn't help
my legs feel better when they tightened up as thirty miles
came and went and I passed the five-hour mark. I'd imagined myself occasionally stopping during the day to gaze
at pleasant vistas along the Charles River, thinking great
thoughts while surges of well-being and accomplishment
filled me. All who saw me would intuitively understand
the magnitude of my achievement. Instead, here I was,
struggling along in total anonymity, no doubt the most
mundane-seeming of pedestrians.

Never had I been so aware of the essential privacy of
the running experience. Instead of runner's high, I was
experiencing what might be called "the incognito effect."
Everything since leaving my apartment that morning had
taken on a double hue. There was what I knew I was
doing, and then there was what anyone observing me
might have *thought* I was doing. I knew I was a hero;
observers saw a dour, dumpy-looking, slowish jogger of

unremarkable proportion. The longer I ran, the wider the gulf between the two became. That much of life operates under a similar principle was little comfort to aching tendons. Was it for this meager insight that I'd set aside the day?

It was continuously, if mildly, irritating to see other runners, in that not even these members of my own tribe stopped to inquire about or marvel at what I was doing—naturally enough, I suppose. I mean, the wisdom of a few hours' distance had allowed me to see the foolishness of having expected any kind of understanding from that clothing store clerk, but surely these actual *runners* ought to pay more respectful attention? Instead, they were ignoring me. Worse, they were passing me! How galling!

Losing flying speed, it was hard not to begin to be obsessed with Finishing This Thing. My vision narrowed, my thoughts shrank. No vistas, no glimpses of far-off buildings, no sociological speculations or psychological breakthroughs. My view closed down mile by mile. As I circled Fresh Pond clockwise, the beautiful reservoir was always available on my right, woods or a golf course, mostly lovely, to my left, but my conscious attention could only just manage the blacktop stretching straight ahead, and then the particular pavement segment three-to-ten-feet directly in front of my steps. The leather toe reinforcement area between black rubber sole and blue nylon shoe upper revealed a fascinating texture to which I'd clearly never paid enough attention.

I began to imagine slowing, slowing, until finally I would stop, terminally absorbed in some minute pebble pattern in the path's surface invisible to anyone else. The appeal of such cessation grew dangerously.

I bumped into a friend on my third lap, and that helped. Ordinary running-talk, what he would do in his next race, what I'd done in my last one, served to distract me and we got through a mile or so not too far above eight-minute pace before parting. That was the good news. The bad news was that the minimal extra effort it had taken just to stay with his graciously-slowed pace, pretty much wiped me out. Margin for error dwindles, then disappears, beyond the marathon distance, and I'd overspent. My break-walk after that lap didn't help much. Nor did mind games like trying to stay an even distance behind a pokey woman who passed me. She pulled away effortlessly. I struggled along, needing an unscheduled rest halfway through that penultimate pond lap. The afternoon was slipping away now, cooling perceptibly as the sun's rays thinned; it wasn't quite the shortest day of the year yet, but would be in a couple of weeks. I was very tight, the lap absurdly long.

The final circuit, by contrast, was comparatively easy. Knowing it was almost over had restored some of the run's elusive magic. Fears of not being able to finish disappeared as the end beckoned just two miles, then one, then less, away. The joy that began to make itself felt was somewhat tempered, as it turned out, by regret that soon I'd be leaving this little world of the run to rejoin the real one. The world of others, of obligations. Still, I was happy slogging towards the finish, and revitalized to be not too far above a nine-minute pace. Happily beat. How wrong I'd been at the outset to consider my start a conservative one!

After six hours and ten minutes, or almost exactly an average of ten minutes per mile covered overall, I ground blissfully to a stop at the Pond's upper parking lot. I wish I could report the thrilling details of the finishing celebration but, appropriately enough, there was no celebration. My wife was waiting with the car, and I simply clambered into the gray Toyota and we went home. Inside of half an hour—such are the birthday indulgences we allow ourselves—I was soaking in a hot bath, enjoying a mighty feeling of satisfaction.

I had worried some, before the run, about how my body would recover, but in fact wasn't beset by any special aches or pains in the next few (very easy) days of running. I noticed a change in attitude, though. My psychological capital had been depleted, and the drive to get out and run was all but gone. A consecutive running streak of a year's length ended within ten days, and my yearly mileage totals were revised downward as December diminished. It seemed somehow pleasingly consistent to me that the after-effects of the run proved to be no more what I'd expected than the run itself. After all, the point had been to pursue the unexpected.

Having had that day for my own purposes, and having made something satisfying out of it, was, to me at least, reward enough. And if others might not see it the way I did ... well, that was the lesson of "the incognito effect," wasn't it? It can't hurt to be reminded from time to time of the necessity of making one's own satisfactions, and of the futility of expecting anyone else to understand them. The gulf between what we feel we're doing and what others perceive us to be doing will remain the most ultra of all distances, one that no amount of miles, or words, can finally bridge.

CHAPTER SIX

AGAINST THE INEVITABLE

Tah-ah-ah-ime. . . is on my sah-ide. . . yes it is!
MICK JAGGER, 1965
(WHAT WOULD HE SAY TODAY?)

IN 1998, WHEN PATRICK, MY older son, began running in the cross country program where I coached (thankfully, in my case, only the girls), our running experiences overlapped hugely and in new ways. The present-tense passages here are me in my mid-fifties, more than a decade ago.

Prologue

Amile into a 2.25 mile race, one knows a lot. Here's what I knew as I passed the familiar faded arrow marker that morning at the Fresh Pond reservoir in Cambridge in September of 1999: I knew I was reasonably comfortable at 6:44, and could probably hold that pace; I knew the crowded race field had stretched out by now, with our small group between a lead pack and another roughly two-thirds of the runners, who were following us; I knew we'd lucked out with a glorious fall morning, only a few puddles here and there left from yesterday's deluge. I knew my fifteen-year-old son, Patrick, was just off my right shoulder, a step behind me.

Here's what I didn't know: I didn't know whether Patrick was going to be able to hold the pace, and I didn't know whether or not I really wanted him to. I mean, after all, if he hung in there, if he stayed right with me—well, he might, in fact, he might, actually, beat me!

And what would that mean? What kind of a contest, exactly, were we engaged in here? We'd both been pointing towards this day, this race, for almost a year, through several trial efforts and not-quites. Who was going to win? What was the prize? If Patrick won, was I somehow "not as good" as he was? If I stayed ahead, did that mean I was a "better" runner? How much was riding on this? In this competition, could there be happy endings all around, or only for one? Was some monstrous generational archetype playing itself out here? Was this our story, or everybody's story? Just over a mile from the end, it wasn't clear yet what kind of a story this was going to turn out to be.

Dramatis Personae

Patrick had come a long way from his first outings as a wobbly, middle school cross country plodder. Last year, as a freshman, he'd dropped six full minutes off his time for the high school's 2.67 mile course during the season, to a respectable 18:35, and he wasn't usually the last runner anymore, a spot he'd held down in virtually every middle school outing. In fact, it was when he'd turned in a time under thirteen minutes for a hilly 3K course near the end of that freshman season that I'd realized it was quite possible he was now —gulp—*faster than Dad!*

Not to say that Dad was particularly fast. I came to running late, after quitting smoking at thirty-one, and never ran on any cross country or track team at any level in school. But I loved it from the first, getting caught up in the Shorter/Rogers/Fixx 1970s boom, and found that I could do reasonably well. I happily trained fifty and sixty miles a week through my thirties, with qualifying for and running Boston Marathons my primary running focus. The year 1981 was probably my best, as I registered a 2:44 marathon PR and also managed to dip just under five minutes for a track mile.

I can get in twenty-five or thirty miles now in a good week, and am not only twenty years beyond my best days as a runner, but twenty pounds beyond them as well. I still love running, though, and am not uncompetitive. At fifty-five, I like to see where I can place in my Fat Old Guys division if I can keep it under seven minute pace for five miles.

So when Patrick's freshman cross country season was over, and he'd taken home one of the team's "Most Improved" awards, I proposed to him a little friendly family competition. Why didn't we go to Fresh Pond some Saturday and see who'd come out ahead in the regular all-comers fun run race? Seemed a good way to extend the season a bit, and to give both of us a little extra incentive. Naturally, things didn't turn out to be quite as simple as we'd thought.

FLASHBACK: THE BIG RACE (TAKE #1)

That November morning when we'd gone to the Pond was brisk enough that we'd both worn tights, but had already warmed enough in the 10:00 AM sun that we shed our jackets before the race. Fresh Pond! Its Saturday morning races (once around for 2.5 miles, twice for five) are an institution, a fixture as basic to any Boston-area runner's universe as the sun or the snow. It was great to introduce Patrick to some of the folks who'd been show-ing up here for years and years: Duke, Dave, Diane, though I didn't get to the Pond often anymore, and may never have known these people in any other context than sweating through runs together. It meant something to all of us that another generation was taking its place. Surely the ghosts of legendary Fresh Pond *racemeister* Fred Brown and a host of others were smiling down on us.

Patrick and I went out together, were at 6:45 for the first mile, and I felt good about his chances, given his

84

fitness level. But it wasn't his day. Despite our warm-up loop, I was the one who knew the terrain and had whatever "home course" advantage might exist. Besides that, Patrick hadn't run much since the JV race in the League meet, nearly three weeks earlier, while I'd had a good final couple of weeks of training. And, just maybe, the idea of Beating Dad made this effort more challenging than a routine race. Whatever the reason, I held pace nicely, hitting two miles in 13:30, while Patrick dropped off and eventually came in almost a minute behind me. This clearly was not a race representative of his actual strength.

Our drive home wasn't a downer, though. In fact, we could chatter freely about the shared race, reviewing it, chewing it over—and it tasted good. Patrick and I had never run together in a serious race before. He'd *watched* my races many times, me smiling after a successful road effort or grinding to the end of a grimly satisfying marathon; I'd been there for his struggles as he learned the ropes of cross country. But now we were entering into each other's experience more fully, sharing the sweat in a way beyond words. Has any runner not felt the kinship of the race experience? The pleasure felt when, half an hour after finishing a marathon, you find yourself in a food line next to the person you ran the middle ten miles with, en route to either PR or disaster? *Hello, old friend!* In Patrick's and my case, kinship already in place, this bond was even stronger, and it felt great.

Was this what Ken Griffey (senior) felt back in 1990, taking the field with his son in Seattle? He'd hit

.377 in twenty-one games after being traded over from Cincinnati to join his son for a career swan song. Did this mean I'd be capable of a sub-13-minute Fresh Pond time, inspired by Patrick's presence? Wow! We made the pledge then that in the spring, after track season, we'd try this racing thing again.

Flashback: The Big Race (Take #2)

A few notes from Patrick's freshman spring track season: on April 13, he came *home from his track meet with news of a 2:47 half mile.* Great, I thought, an eleven second improvement over his previous PR established last weekend. Ouch, I thought, I don't know if I could run a 2:47 today if someone with a gun were chasing me. Three weeks later he'd peaked with a 2:39 half, as well as recording a 6:01 mile. Again *great*; again *ouch!* He was psyched for our rematch as soon as his season ended. I was wondering whether I could even stick close enough to make things halfway competitive.

I snuck over to the Pond one Saturday to check for life signs and see where I stood. Amazingly, I ran pretty well, actually hanging near my fall pace for most of the race. Maybe the old guy hadn't lost it yet, or not *entirely*, anyhow. Maybe I could hold the kid off for another season. Trotting around on a cool down lap after the race, I was chatting with a fellow who'd been with me for some of the race before pulling away. He was a friendly guy, down from Vermont, Mike Sullivan by name, and he chuckled as he listened to my hopeful thoughts about staying ahead of the offspring.

"Well," he said, "don't count on staying ahead of 'em—in my case, it was my daughter. I didn't feel threatened when she decided to quit soccer and take up cross country instead, but she turned out to be pretty fast."

Whoops! I'll say she did. Turns out Mike was the father of two-time national Foot Locker cross country champion *Erin Sullivan*! My sense of optimism for maintaining parental primacy melted away. The inevitable was near. The next generation will always, in the end, win. But what does that victory mean for the defeated older generation? Scanning my memory for intergenerational archetypes I kept finding images of Acrisius struck dead by the discus thrown his son Perseus, or of Darth Vader, battered, dying in Luke Skywalker's arms. No, things didn't look good.

I was certainly reconciled to being defeated, if that was the way it had to be. On the other hand, I didn't want to go quietly. In late May, as Patrick's season wound down, I returned to Fresh Pond for a final tune-up, discovering along the way that the course had changed, shortened by construction to something closer to 2.25 miles. I panted to a 15:06, about the equivalent of what I'd done in the fall 2.5 miler on the original course. At least, if Patrick won, he'd not be beating a totally out of shape Old Guy. I was concerned about being a challenge to him, about representing well enough a standard worthy of beating.

As it turned out, I needn't have worried—Patrick tripped while on a charity walk event at the end of the month, fracturing his elbow, and went to receive another "most-improved" award at his track banquet that very night wearing a sporty new sling. The race was off, at least for the foreseeable future, and the issue was now when he could resume training. Of course, any postponement of our competition ultimately would work in Patrick's favor. Could I in fact keep a level of fitness while he recuperated and trained his way back to his May condition?

This delay actually took the pressure off of any summer confrontations, and rather than approaching the summer as rivals, it turned out that I was trying to help Patrick back to fitness. We did a couple of five-mile-ish Cape Cod summer road races together, in one starting behind the entire field of hundreds and working our way up through most of the pack at a workout pace; in the other, trying to keep a 7:15-ish pace from the start. Both runs were great experiences, as Patrick became more comfortable with the road-race scene. He wasn't stressed about regaining his track conditioning, and I didn't worry, knowing that once he hit cross country season again he'd be getting plenty of work.

And what about me? My own fitness level hovered at the same OK-for-short-races-at-below-seven-minute-pace level. I remember, years ago, reading about the great Henry Rono checking his fitness by monitoring pulse levels, and recalled my own calculations, in my marathoning days, based on whether my morning resting pulse was mid-forties or low fifties, and on how short my recoveries could be between hard quarters during a track session. Now I have other ways to check my fitness: when I squeeze into my 36 waist Docker khakis without cutting off my breathing or developing bladder symptoms, for example, I know I'm headed in the right direction.

The longer our confrontation was delayed, the more I felt myself hanging on. The race against Patrick had turned into a struggle not against him, but against my own deterioration. In essence, I'd be racing against my own capabilities, which is, of course, what all racers do all the time. In the single circuit of Fresh Pond, I'd be battling on several fronts, and so would everyone else. No one else would see Patrick taking on Dad in some epic confrontation, no one else would know that I was trying to hold back some generational stopwatch. If we were being Darth Vader and Luke Skywalker, it would only be in our own private movie, and there are always as many movies as there are runners.

FINALE—THE BIG DAY (AT LAST)

A few weeks into Patrick's sophomore cross country training, as the first meet approached, I sensed that the time had come, and set a mid-September date. My wife, ever the concerned Mom, asked me the morning we were scheduled to go out whether Patrick was really ready. Was I pushing things too fast? Would this be too stressful? *For whom, I wondered?* My own concerns centered on falling apart myself if we waited much longer. The point, after all, wasn't to create a situation in which we were certain of the outcome before the race even began! A *certain* victory: for either of us, that wouldn't be a *real* victory.

We pulled into my usual parking spot, right where we'd landed the previous November for the first try at this. We were both pretty wired, and I was on the lookout for omens of any sort. Unfortunately, the tape player gave me not "Rocky," but old Tom Petty groaning out "Echo." *You just got tired, you just gave in.* Not exactly what I needed, and both of us smiled nervously as we stretched and jogged off towards the park.

Unexpectedly, we found a huge crowd of people milling about at the starting line in the lower parking lot. It looked as though four or five local cross country teams had decided to make this a last pre-season test, so with the usual crowd in place as well, there had to be more than one hundred runners, probably the largest field I'd seen in a couple of decades of racing at The Pond. Warming up, we trotted out to the 3/4 mile mark, visited my usual bushes for a pre-race pit stop (one must, after all, pass along *all* of the traditions), and returned to the start, doing a couple of pick-ups over the last half-mile. Then it was time.

At the command, we were off, my elbows out wide to fend off the mob, Patrick in my wake, watching our steps literally as well as figuratively. By the quarter mile mark (1:38) things had thinned out enough that I could relax a bit, and shortly thereafter we were a small pack behind clusters in front and behind. We seemed comfortably on schedule (3:18) at the half, and my mile split of 6:44 was fine. Fine for me, at any rate—but what about Patrick? This was where he'd dropped off last time ....

Not today. He hung tough and as I looked for the one-and-a-half mile marker, he moved up and went past me on my right, running strongly. Now I had to check the tank to see what was left. I was the one hanging on at this point, but I made sure Patrick knew I wasn't going away, grunting to him that we had just over a half mile left.

The Fresh Pond course is flat, except for the quarter mile heading up to the upper parking lot and the two-mile mark, where there are two small but annoying little hills. And that's where Patrick sealed his win, gaining a few crucial strides on each rise while I struggled back between them. We hit two miles in 13:36 and 13:38, and just had the downhill stretch to the lower lot to negotiate. How many different rationales can fill a runner's mind over the closing moments of a race! Pushing to the end at below six-minute pace, we'd come a long way from Patrick's first baby steps, but that was the kind of excitement I felt filling me. And what could he have been feeling? I imagined a salad of desperation and glee as he fought to maintain his edge and the cherished victory rushed towards him.

Had this race taken fifteen minutes, or a year? Or was it nearly fifteen years, since those first steps? Or the fifty-plus years of my own wayward life? Whatever the case, this was surely a highlight film clip moment for both of us. I wanted a band. I wanted film lights, cameras running, reporters taking notes on this once-in-a-lifetime event. I wanted the freeze frame, the champagne, laurel wreaths all around. . . .

What I got was a worn tongue depressor with the number 14 written on it as I passed the finish in 15:07. Patrick had beaten me to the line in 15:05 for stick number 13. The torch was passed! I'd never felt so happy to finish behind someone.

Postscript

My reward for not being faster was Patrick's complete and utter pleasure in beating me. He'd been just as invested in the race as I was. My own sense of fulfillment was complete, too—I'd won a victory of sorts over the forces of decrepitude by giving him a good race. It was two very happy runners who jogged back to the car and drove home. He went on to lower his time below the eighteen minute mark for the cross country course over the next few weeks; I was slowed by knee pains and a month later was pretty much in a total rest-and-recovery phase.

Patrick and I have given something up: we no longer have The Race to look forward to and plan around. On the other hand, we have gained some things, too. While I certainly haven't lost a son, nor Patrick a father, we've each gained a colleague, a fellow runner in a new and deeper sense of shared experience. We have gained The Race as memory, as an indelible tape to replay and savor on the mind's VCR. We've gained an answer to a thorny question: what does it mean to "do well?" The waiting, the race, and the aftertaste of it all served to provide that answer, not in words, but in feelings. When the question is asked, to either son or father in this case, he can reply, with conviction and with a smile, "What does it mean to do well? Yes, I know something about that. Let me tell you. It's like that time. . ."

You can't avoid the inevitable, but sometimes, when you hug it, it feels mighty good.

CHAPTER SEVEN

GOING FOR THE ALL-GEEZER TEAM

*No man ever followed his genius till it misled him.
Though the result were bodily weakness, yet perhaps no
one can say that the consequences were to be regretted,
for these were a life in conformity to higher principles.*

THOREAU, WALDEN

MY STORIES OF THESE SHORT age-group efforts in road
races seem to me an ultrarunning chapter, since running
all one's life is the real ultramarathon.

My goodness, it's a lovely day! I'm running easily through gorgeous leafy suburban Concord, Massachusetts, surrounded by fleet, fit females as we hit the first mile mark in the 2005 version of the local Fourth of July five-mile road race in something like 6:50. It's a treat to be running with Karin, Cricky, Lindsey, and Emma—the core of our high school's second-in-the-state cross country team. And as a sixty-year-old coot I savor all the more this rare chance to run with some of the girls I coach in the fall. Ah, life is sweet. . . but. . . but, damn it, I have an *agenda*. The girls are larking, gabbing, and into a fun outing, while I, well, I'm a tad behind schedule, and have to get a move on, because, *gulp,* I want—it's hard to admit this, but—I want to WIN today. *Win*, you ask? Win? Um, come in *first?* What about that crowd of runners ahead of you?

OK, OK, here's the thing: I harbor no illusions about jetting up to the race leaders, who are already nearly two minutes ahead of me after a mile. But I do want to win my *age group*, which I believe I can do with a sub-34-minute time (last year's 60+ winner clocked a 33:44, a time I'd bettered back in April in winning a Lexington five-miler). So, and hate to say it, but girls, I gotta go! I have, if only to myself, promises to keep, and at least four more miles to go before—well, whatever.

A brief historical refresher: I didn't start running until I gave up smoking at thirty-one and sort of spontaneously broke into a trot a couple of months later. The trot grew into a habit; you runners know the story. The runner then gets curious about racing as he feels himself getting into shape, and so on. I was doing this in the mid-1970s (with a few million others—no pioneer I!), and I was young and strong and all was right with the world, at least, with the running world. I loved it, and I even got pretty good at it, though there were so many better runners around I hardly noticed my own prowess. It was personally thrilling, sure, to be under twenty-eight minutes for five miles, but I was one of a crowd. Breaking 2:50 for a marathon was a worthy achievement, but only what anyone had to do to run the Boston Marathon, and thousands did it. It was exciting to plan, and then to run, a sub-five-minute mile, but since more people finished ahead of me than behind me in that mile test event I'd orchestrated, my satisfactions were personal and didn't include any notion of general . . . *victory.*

Victory. Finishing first. Going faster than everyone else. That was not on the menu, it seemed, no matter how good I got as a runner. And I never even really thought about it. I generally ran with people who were good runners, clearly faster runners than I, and I simply never expected to beat them. I knew who the best racers in my club, Cambridge Sports Union, were, and I wasn't among them. Then there were the heavy hitters from gangs like the Greater Boston Track Club. Whew! Forget about competing with *them!* And of course, one constantly read about the superstars of running, the Seb Coes and the Steve Scotts and the Mary Slaneys and the Joan

Benoits. One could be inspired, but one didn't actually dream of doing what they did, which was—over and over—*winning.*

Besides, my arc of progress was inevitably slowing, and finally stopping. After nearly a decade of running, it began to dawn on me that PRs hadn't been coming along much. In fact, they hadn't been coming at all! My 27:16 for five miles at age thirty-six was—I swallowed hard and had to admit after a few years— going to be it. In 1983, the year of my older son Patrick's birth, I plummeted from a 2:50-ish Boston to being a basic non-runner for months after his arrival. My plans for a comeback in 1984 were grand, but came to nothing, as I struggled (and often failed) to get in training *months* that matched the seventy or eighty mile *weeks* I'd put in a few years earlier. As I turned forty, I had a one-year-old son, and was way out of the training-for-marathons business. But having a baby around wasn't the whole problem. I also found cranky tendons, cranky back, and general bodily crankiness becoming more the norm than the exception. I got in a few races over the next few years, but second son Eamonn's arrival when I was 42 basically knocked me out of *any* racing at all. I never stopped running. That would have been unthinkable! But I was a very different runner than I had been a decade before.

My earliest foray into age-group racing, in a 1985 hometown three-miler in Connecticut, was symbolic. I'd actually gotten in some sporadic training, had some speed left, and felt as though I could run hard and have a shot at a masters (over age 40) win. I ran well, a 16:41 for second place overall, the closest I've ever come to actually winning a race outright, in fact. Amazing, really, and more a testament to the residue of years of hard training than to any then-current work. I felt pretty darn good, I can tell you, ready to have my ego boosted by recognition in front of my old neighbors and my family as I strode up to receive whatever massive trophy would surely be mine. But as it turned out, the one guy who finished (five seconds) ahead of me was forty, too, and was generously handed both the winner's trophy— and the master's winner's trophy! I watched in fuming disbelief as a train of others came forward to get their age-group prizes, me empty-handed, seething, the odd man out.

As I hit fifty in late 1994, I thought I could get my running act together again. I was in a steady job situation, sharing baby-management with my wife had become much-easier sharing of boy-management, and I aimed to see what I had left, working back to a steadier (if more modest) training scheme of 30-35 mile weeks. Whereas I had no regular running log for 1985, my 1995 log (just purchasing one was a sign of hope) shows that I had enough left to turn in a 30:55 five-miler in Lexington on Patriots' Day, then push to a 14:59 two-and-a-half miler—yikes, six-minute pace!— the following Saturday at the regular Fresh Pond race. Okay, I was actually called by some running club mates

and recruited to be on their fifty-plus team in the following weekend's James Joyce Ramble 10K. So my
forties hadn't seen me emerge as an age-group star, but
my time was here at last!

A week later I'd banged up my Achilles tendon suf-
ficiently to shelve me for nearly a month en route to a
disappointing 40:55 10K during which I did neither the
team nor myself any good and should doubtless have
dropped out instead of hanging in only to worsen my
injury. The temptations of age-group glory had done me
in. The same year, I started coaching the girls' cross country team at the high school where I teach, and discovered
something all coaches know: coaching is not good for
one's own training.

Finally, as I approached sixty, I thought again about
trying to make an age-group splash. Just in time, too, as
that's about it on the age-group front: most road races
have masters (40-49) and veterans (50-59) categories,
then slide to whatever they call age sixty and above. If
it didn't work out this time, in other words, there was
not going to be a chance later to mix it up with the sep-
tuagenarians or octogenarians separately. I was already
in their camp. (This isn't true for events like national
track competitions; there one finds age groups right on
up in five-year denominations, so one could, for example, take part in the 400-meter race for 75-79-year-olds.
But ninety-nine percent of local road races figure—
correctly, I'm sure—that giving age-group awards for
groups who are unlikely to participate in measurable
numbers would be silly.)

So, as 2005 dawned, there I was: training about twenty-five miles a week less than in my heyday, and weighing about twenty-five pounds more. Not an ideal combination. On the other hand, I was sixty, a bona fide oldster, and ready to go to work. I began to ratchet my mileage back up into the thirties from the lows to which it had dropped as I coached in the fall, and worked to peel off some poundage. The All-Geezer team beckoned!

What follows is the story of my quest. Some highs, some lows, some surprises, and some lessons. For whatever they're worth, and for whatever amusement they afford my fellow runners, I offer them here. One man's quixotic search for WMDs—i.e. Wins in My Division.

Race #1: February— Super 5K, Lowell

Either I wasn't ready, or no age-group race opportunity presented itself in January, probably both! I had decided to begin my trophy-hunting career at a race I'd done a year before to mark progress in my early my weight-loss and re-conditioning efforts, an event on February sixth (Super Bowl Sunday) called the Super 5K, in nearby Lowell. I did get in a local fun run 2.5 miler at Cambridge's Fresh Pond a couple of weeks before that event as a kind of tune-up, and did that in 16:44, which I felt OK about, given that it was my first race in a long time and was over a snow-packed course in places. I felt pretty good, in fact, and looked forward to a solid race in a couple of weeks—solid enough, at least, I thought, to be a factor in my age group.

Race day turned out to be warmish for February. I actually was regretting wearing my winter tights, and took off a couple of top layers to race in just a t-shirt with them. I wanted to be fairly aggressive, hoping to get near twenty minutes and bag a WMD, so I went out reasonably hard. I could see a guy who clearly was in my age group—and hoped maybe he wouldn't be able to quite so clearly tell that I was an age-group rival, in case that helped me sneak past him. But I was definitely in a most-competitive mindset. He was moving along pretty darn well! I tucked in behind him, and also noticed in our group another possible Old Guy, and a couple of women-folk—one a young girl, in fact, who was running along effortlessly, it seemed. She looked like a middle schooler. Geez, she'd surely fade!

I'd checked the previous year's results and seen that the winner in the 60+ group had done a 20:21. I'd been pleased enough with my own 22:02 then, as a kind of starting point on what I hoped would be a journey back to competitive fitness. I knew I could beat my own last year's time, and thought I could be somewhere around the previous winner's time. And now it seemed as though I was probably running along with that guy, or some version of him. We passed the mile in 6:18, which seemed, simply, too fast! Oh no! Had I blown it and been too aggressive? Who was going to fall apart first in our little flotilla? There was indeed a bit of jockeying and position-shifting, but, rather surprisingly, no one crashed and burned, and we all kept together.

And we all finished within ten seconds. First, the woman, who won the women's overall in 20:22, and next (wow!), the thirteen-year-old, in 20:25. The fast start appeared to have taken anyone's ability to kick away, and we crossed in the line we'd been in for the last mile-plus. First across in our division was the previous year's winner, 68-year-old Bill Spencer of New Hampshire, in 20:28, followed by 62-year-old Joe Drugan in 20:30, and 60-year-old me in 20:32. So much for kicking age-group butt! So much for things being less competitive in my new division! WMD's were no easier to find for me than they were for the Americans in Iraq! I'd run a pretty darn good race and been beaten by two older guys and two younger women! Yikes!

I *did* take home a trophy—a little statuette of a football player (get it, Super 5K on Super Bowl Sunday?). And I did have the satisfaction of having cut a minute and a half off of my previous year's time, as well as hearing various wows murmured about the fast competitive oldsters. But, coupled with my memories of dashed age-group hopes in earlier decades, I admit that overall I wasn't as happy as I'd hoped to be on the way home. My campaign was underway, but I'd gotten my first lesson, too.

> **Lesson #1:** Serious racing, whatever age you are, whatever your goal, is HARD. Sometimes we need a visceral reminder of even the most obvious of truths.

Race #2: March—
An Ras Mor, Cambridge

I was a little nervous about this one at the Gaelic named
event. The race seemed like a bigger one than the Super
5K, so things might get even tighter. I didn't feel especially sharp. In fact, a treadmill session about ten days
earlier had left me with some sort of hamstring strain as
I got too ambitious trying to put in some hard miles or
halves. What else is there to do on a treadmill, anyhow?
The snowy winter had left me on the treadmill a few
times, and also using cross-country skiing (as I learned to
skate-ski—not well, but it was fun and certainly a workout!) in place of running. The day before the race, in
fact, I'd been out during a damp snow skiing on my very
own street!

I hoped that, with modest expectations and a more
modest start, I might be able to improve or at least
match my 20:32. I meant to coddle my iffy leg with
a slow build-up and then hope to get into a groove of
some sort. And the race felt pretty good at the start,
actually. They'd had to adjust the course somewhat
after the previous day's snow and some late construction work, but we basically ran from somewhere around
MIT up to Harvard Square and then back down, mostly
on Mass. Ave., so I had a rough sense of the halfway
point, anyhow, even if no actual mile markers. I felt,
at about two miles, as though I was having a pretty
good race, but that's as specific as it got. As my watch
neared twenty minutes I kept pushing, and we seemed
to be getting back home, but as twenty passed and

twenty-one came, and we didn't turn into the area I thought meant the finish, I got nervous. Damn! Had I screwed up somehow? Twenty-two minutes! Where the heck was the finish line?? Twenty-THREE minutes?? Another turn. OK, I could see where we were headed now, but this is no 5K distance! TWENTY-FOUR!! How bad was this, anyhow? I drove myself, enraged, to a 24:37, pretty totally bummed, and drifted achingly away from the finish afterwards sharing complaints with my fellow sufferers. The common theme was "That was no 5K" expressed in fatigued frustration.

After a light cool-down, as much needed mentally as physically, I found my way to some posted results. They'd conceded that their calculations of the last-minute course changes were (considerably) off, and were calling it a 3.6 mile race now—only an extra half mile! I thought the new distance still seemed short given how I'd felt. Those hadn't seemed like 6:50s I was running! But my mood lightened fast when I saw a little number 1 next to my name, before the 60-69 notation. I had done it! Victory! Better yet, two places behind me I saw another number 1 and realized that I'd have won the 50-59 category as well as my own. Ah, sweetness and bliss. WMD! My new favorite race.

Along with my small trophy (still small, but at least a runner on it instead of a football player this time, no more Heisman jokes at home) I received a check for forty dollars. Wow, there went my amateur status and Olympic eligibility! My ride home felt much better than it had from Lowell the previous month.

Lesson #2: There was a lesson here as well, a useful one for road racers of any age: Expect The Unexpected.

Race # 3: April—
Patriots' Day Five Miler, Lexington

I remembered this one somewhat. When I'd stopped marathoning years before, I'd done this Patriots' Day classic at least once. It bills itself as the fourth-oldest road race in New England, and draws a pretty big field; there were over 450 finishers this year. I didn't remember any big hills, but maybe I'd just repressed them, or maybe I was in good enough shape still then that I hadn't noticed stuff that now would bring me low. I ran into some familiar faces from my years on the roads here, and had some pleasant chats. Well, OK, not ALL of my chat with Bob Reagan was pleasant, in that he looked me over, after hearing I'd hit the 60s, and opined, "Gee, Tom, I don't know quite how to say this, heh-heh, but gee, if you lost some weight you could really do well in this division!" The unthinking judgment of the naturally skinny! Thanks, Bob!

I forgot about Bob once the race began, though, and instead focused on Duke Hutchinson up ahead. I knew he'd be competitive in the 50's age group, and thought I could use him as a target/pacer. After a pretty good-feeling 6:37 opening mile, that strategy seemed a good one. Two miles in 13:20 felt good, too.

I'd been biking into work more—no big trek, but the round trip couldn't be hurting my fitness level as an add-on. I'd also gotten out to the track for the first time in years, and had gotten in a few modest speedwork sessions (repeat quarters in the mid-eighties with quarter jog-rests). Once or twice a week I might also get in a short routine with light free weights at home, too, and along with these I was doing some of the ab-circuit routines the girls' cross country team does. I was, I have to admit, actually getting into shape!

I missed the three-mile checkpoint, but hit four in 27:04, and, more important, though tired, I still had some strength left and could maintain pace. I knew pretty much where we were (no new course adjustments this time), and turning into the final (downhill and flat, thankfully) half mile I could push with some confidence, so push I did, and crossed the line in 33:25—a solid five miles!

And a solid division win, too! Take that, skinny Bob! No fifties-group win this time, with Duke, fifth or sixth in that category, in a good fifteen or twenty seconds ahead of me, but I didn't care at all. This was a good time in a big race, and I was plenty happy. My trophy this month was in fact huge, matching my happiness. I went home to watch the marathon on TV, feeling I'd earned that pleasure fully. Whether you're sixteen or sixty, working out gets you into better condition. Hardly shocking wisdom, but exactly what I'd let slip from my consciousness as I meandered through middle age, spending as much time and energy thinking about what I *couldn't* do any more as a runner as I did planning for what I *could* do.

> **Lesson #3:** A simple one: Basically, WORK ALWAYS PAYS OFF.

Races # 4 and 5, May and June

A much smaller race—the Parker School Five-Mile Classic in nearby Devens—was on my plate for May. Somehow, with various days ruled out for preparations related to one son's high school graduation and picking up another as his college year ended, this seemed to have to be the weekend for a race, and this seemed to be the race. I liked that it was not far from home, and I admit that I also liked the idea of a "breather" in my campaign. This race seemed to draw around 100 folks each year, and my researches into past editions on the Cool Running website didn't turn up what appeared to be threats to my two-race long "win streak."

Wrong again, Tom. First I ran into problems just GETTING to the race, as the related two-miler seemed to be in progress as I drove up, preventing me from parking where I wanted to. Also, I'd stupidly forgotten my watch as I left home—not a good omen. Furthermore, as I circled around finding a parking spot finally, I couldn't help noticing that I was going up and down quite a bit. Hills? And let's see, what else—oh, yes, the gray skies opened as race time approached, and we headed out into a downpour. Was I having fun yet?

Most distressing of all, there was no doubt that, as we went off, I was in the company of a grizzled bunch, a fleet of gnarled veterans who sure looked like they might be—gulp—in my age group! Geez. Wasn't that guy, could it be, one of my fellow oldsters from Lowell? Hey! This was supposed to be a breather, guys, and now here I am, watchless and wet, hanging onto a crowd as I slog my heavy, rain-soaked shoes towards a finish still miles and hills away. Suddenly I realized that a new mindset had replaced the one I'd known throughout my earlier racing years. My successes of recent months had subtly altered my outlook. I had come here not just to run well, but to WIN. This was new, and this wasn't one-hundred percent good. I felt a kind of—*pressure,* previously unknown.

But, all's well that ends well, and I pushed hard, pulled away from that pack, and finished in a mushy-but-respectable 34:24. I saw my bunch stream in for the next minute or two. It turned out in the end that there was quite a group of 60s guys there; on this day the top five in my division would have won the mysteriously weak fifties division! *You go, geezers!* My winner's trophy had been harder to come by than I had expected, but that made it simply sweeter. Still, I had surprised myself with my attitude, and had to do some thinking about that. Was I putting myself into a position where no WMD actually meant having a bad race? Where *only* by winning, or by doing really well, could I be satisfied? That didn't seem like a good thing. Certainly it is exactly what as a coach I preach *against*. Racing would be a poor thing indeed if only winners succeeded!

That attitude issue accompanied me to my June race, the big Bunker Hill five-miler in Boston. Also coming along were 90-degree temperatures and heavy humidity. Ugh! I wasn't focused on the nasty weather, though. After all, everyone would have to face the same conditions. I figured if I could get back below 34 minutes, I might win this one, too, to head into my major goal race of the year (next month's hometown five-miler) on a four-race, win-streak high. I was actually kind of cocky as I warmed up, imagining my name being called and strolling up to accept my richly-deserved trophy. I picked out a guy at the start who might have been my age and who appeared pretty fit, and imagined letting him pace me for a couple of miles before pulling away.

And pace me he did, as the first mile passed in 6:35. Didn't feel all that bad, either, but I was a tad concerned—after all, that was a bit faster than my Lexington split and on a day that clearly wasn't going to permit PRs for anyone. I tried to get into a slightly slower groove, and had no trouble doing that, as the second mile, featuring a long climb up Bunker Hill, went by in just over seven minutes; 13:39 was our split. It was during the third mile that I knew that I wasn't really controlling my own pace anymore. I was simply slowing—another 7-minute mile, and at this point I also knew that I couldn't keep up even *that* pace. There had been another hill, not huge but a hill, in that third mile, and we appeared headed to loop around up Bunker Hill again. Arrgh! Not fun!

My mental calculations, such as I was able to accomplish in my wilting state, told me that, far from breaking

34 minutes on this day, I probably wasn't going to be able to hang in for even a sub-35. I imagined staggering in with about a 37 or so, possibly dropping dead on arrival. These so-called calculations in fact did me in completely, and after three miles I did what most runners have done at one point or another and what all runners hate: I stopped! Why go on with a crummy time? Why go on and get no trophy? Weren't times and trophies the most important things?

Arrggh! So much for my pre-race conceit and pride! I jogged wearily back through the streets, returning to the start/finish area as some mid-pack finishers arrived.

There went my win streak, and the ponderings about new pressures as an age-group competitor I'd felt a bit the previous month now loomed even more hugely. Why had I gone out that recklessly (as in retrospect I so clearly had)? Why not a calm 6:50 or so, and a steady try just to beat 35 minutes and my competition? My ego and my expectations had blocked out my sense!

Worse yet, when I eventually checked the web for results that night, I saw that if, instead of jogging back, I'd just jogged on in from my c. 20:30 three-mile split in, say, nine-to-ten-minute miles, *I'd have actually brought home another WMD trophy, since the winner finished in over forty minutes*! I'd blown it from every single standpoint!

So: getting into my winning mindset had made me blind and stupid. And that realization was going to be what I took into my target race for the year, rather than a triumph. OK, then that's what I had to learn from, I guess.

Lesson # 4: Run the race circumstances dictate, not the race your ego has led you to fantasize about.

Race #6: July—
Patriot Classic Five Miler, Concord

So back to my sunny holiday ramble, and the need to pull away from my better-looking, but differently-motivated traveling companions. I worked a bit harder, and did pull away, though the two-mile 13:40-ish split showed that my pushing had simply allowed me to maintain pace through the only mile in the race with anything like hills. I gained a bit more in the third mile, helped no doubt by running right behind my son Eamonn, and hit four miles in about 27:20. I'd have to close with my fastest mile of the race to break 34:00 now, and was struggling. No more rhapsodizing on the glorious day at this point! I'd done a decent job of banking down the competitive fires coming into the race, but the fact was, this hometown five-miler was the biggie for me. There'd be time for another race or two over the summer, probably, but with coaching coming around again late next month and school starting up soon after that, my focus was bound to slip away. This was the race I most wanted. This was the race I'd really pointed towards.

FOCUS! I didn't know who was doing what up ahead, and certainly couldn't see any geezer-targets to go after.

FOCUS! I was doing everything I could to stretch it out, to keep my leg turnover going. I knew very well where I was in relation to the finish line, and what I had to do.

FOCUS! Down to the last turn onto Stow Street, two long blocks to go, the watch moving on relentlessly.

Pumpthump*ungh*! Pumpthump*ungh*! Pumpthump*ungh*! Can I get my weary legs to push me to that onrushing finish line before the big digital clock clicks twice more. *Ungh!* 33:58 *Ungh!* 33:59. DONE!

When the results were taped up for all to see, about a half-hour later, I was inordinately grumpy that they'd clocked me at exactly 34:00, but I was very happy to see that I'd come just over a minute ahead of the second-place Old Guy (the previous year's winner, actually) and had the victory I most wanted.

I might have had a better shot at another mid-33:00's time if I'd been a little more aggressive at the start. But I'd run a solid outing and had won the race I'd most pointed for. Maybe this meant I was getting smarter at last? Apparently not, as my next effort showed..

Race #7: July (again)— Sugar Bowl 5-miler, Boston

I stuck this one into the mix late for a couple of reasons. Mainly, I was greedy to keep racing a lot while things were going well, and this race, seventeen days after the Concord one and two weeks before the Newburyport 5K that was to be my August finale, seemed well-positioned.

Also, I'd done it a couple of times before, in the early 1990s while coming up to entering my fifties then, and giving so-so, not-very-actively-racing-type performances. I found no records of them in my spotty non-logs of that era. I also wanted to get into a BIG race to see what things looked like. I knew there had to be more competition out there, and this one definitely qualified on that score, with fields around 1500!

As the race approached, though, I was less than enthusiastic. My weight had been creeping up—a summer trend, given looser schedules, more room for lunches, and so on. Heavier is not better. Furthermore, we'd been in a stretch of very hot & muggy weather—race day turned out to be slightly better than average for this stretch, but that simply meant humidity nearer 80 than 90, and temperatures of nearly, instead of above, 90. My pokey time at Concord and my disaster at the Bunker Hill race were on my mind as I stood at the airless-feeling start, the asphalt parking lot of Bayside Expo, amid a huge crowd.

I'll spare you the details, and just note that my high-34-minute time felt respectable given the conditions (and given my own apparently slipping condition), and that my streak of wins (at least in completed races) ended. I settled for a second-place trophy, and it wasn't even close: I was *over four minutes* behind oldster winner Colin McCardle's 30-and-change time! Guess my goal of finding some competition at the bigger race had been fulfilled! (Except that in this competition he had been so far ahead I'd never even glimpsed him!?)

And as I dragged my race-battered body around for the next couple of weeks, it became clear that the July 4 accomplishment represented a kind of high-water mark (yearly goal achieved), and that the July 21 race was a mistake, but not one I could simply acknowledge and move past! I'd overdone it, and wasn't sure I could recapture the focus that marked the months from February through June. And therein lay another lesson. The energy—physical and, just as important, mental and emotional—I'd channeled into building for and winning the July 4 race came at a price, and I didn't have the resources—again, physical, mental, or emotional—to keep training and racing at that level. Modest though 6:40-type pace might seem, to prepare for it and execute it over a period of months had left at least this particular geezer gasping. I acknowledged to myself that I might just have found my last WMD.

> **Lesson # 5**: Focus giveth, and focus taketh away.

RACE #8: AUGUST— BEVERLY YANKEE HOMECOMING 5K

Well, um, ahhh, *OK!* That was my reaction after running not as well as I might have, but well enough to win again, in a 20:43 time that actually represented a slight slowdown from my February Lowell 5K. I started cautiously, having warmed carefully without testing what had become a chronic hamstring tightness through any prolonged striding, and as I built to a steady pace, I could indeed feel those darned tightnesses ready to jump out and grab me. This led me to that doubt-full head that often spells disaster, as I mulled whether dropping out was the thing to do, and so on. I got through the first mile, in 6:29, and given the short distance, decided to try to tough it out if the legs didn't really protest significantly. And, luckily, they didn't. This may have been due to a slowing for mile number two to something more like 6:50—some rolling terrain— nothing serious, but the race was thinning out now (the start had been crowded—about 400+ runners), and I was slipping past people rather than being passed, so I wasn't panicking. I did, however, try consciously to maintain and even perhaps pick it up over the last mile-plus, and managed to do so. As we turned down into the park for the finish I found enough to stretch it out more. I wasn't worried by then that I'd trigger race-ending leg issues. No sub-20, though, and I was aware even as I crossed that I'd not matched the Lowell time.

So: why had six months of racing and paying attention left me no better off than I'd been in February? First, the leg issues were real, and in a way I was lucky to get in a race at all, to say nothing of a decent one that took my age group. (Related to this, of course, I hadn't really been able to train effectively for the past couple of weeks, even though I kept getting in my miles.) Second, there *is* a difference between a hot summer race and one on a perfect crisp 50-plus-degree February mid-day. The fact is, I had just gotten kind of stale, and even though I squeezed out

one more race—and another WMD at a Labor Day 5K—
the end of my time of intense focus had definitely arrived.
I'd planned back at the beginning of the year to train
hard and race hard through the summer, but coaching
was coming up in a few weeks, and teaching, too, soon
after that. My story, my year of exploring winning, was
coming to its inevitable end. Which led me to realize:

> **Lesson # 6:** Recognize when you're ready
> to rest.

And rest I did, from my minor-league version of serious training and racing, anyhow. School began, and
coaching began, and, as usual, I found plenty to do even
without getting to road races. That was that, and, well—
dare I ask, *so what?*

You've undoubtedly noticed that the lessons I've mentioned hardly seem revolutionary insights. Turns out
that the whole effort was like that: nothing exactly *new*,
but rather everything seen with an intensity that gave it
freshness. Paying more attention to my running, I saw
why our running rewards attention. In my fourth decade
of going out for a run I saw that it was still very possible
to learn, about running, about limits, about myself.

The trophies, ribbons, plaques (and even one shiny
wristwatch, featuring a drawing of Concord's North
Bridge) from my search for WMDs have found a home of
sorts on a corner bench in my basement office. From the
vantage point of a full year, I admire them fondly when
I occasionally notice them. The real legacy of my efforts,

however, is in my continued desire to run, with the re-newed knowledge that there's a vast well of challenge and satisfaction waiting for anyone in running whenever one chooses to actively engage it. And that, whether at sixty or twenty-six, can only be a good thing.

CHAPTER EIGHT

Do You Run?

Start slowly, then taper off.

WALT STACK, *INDEFATIGABLE WEST COAST
ULTRARUNNING LEGEND, 1960S THROUGH 1980S*

WHEN YOU WAIT MONTHS FOR a particular run, it can spell problems, as seen in this account of a mile run in mid-2010, a year and a half after my lung removal; this is the "all-out" effort I'd begun to plan back in Chapter Two.

Are you a runner? Do you run? What makes someone a runner? I can run. I could run from a burning building, make a dash to catch a closing subway door, run down a block to beat the strolling meter maid to my parked car. I can't, however, run for a mile without stopping to catch my breath.

Thirty-plus years ago, when I found myself mired in self-castigation because I wasn't as dedicated to my running goals as I imagined I should have been, I exhaled a yogic breath of letting go and allowed to myself that I was just a normal runner like everyone else and that that was OK (see Chapter One). In retrospect, it was easy for me to let down my defenses and go easy on myself while still within a context of daily running, in the midst of a streak of years of averaging over fifty miles a week on the roads. My current week's total of running (running here meaning schlumping along for a minute or two slightly faster than a brisk walk, something that doesn't happen on many of my walks) might add up to about a single mile—and that's a big week for me! Weeks go by without my ever breaking out of my happy pokey ambling walk. A few minutes' slow steady trotting now leaves me breathless and gasping.

That being the case, why would I be standing on the starting line at our local high school's track, waiting for the gun to fire in the Newcomers Mile race?

Well, I can at least report that I wasn't altogether happy about being there! I admit to feeling a bit self-conscious, especially considering the field of hard-core, serious athletes surrounding me at the line. My wife Christopher was there, another nervous miling novice, really simply to support me, bless her. There were two or three other moms-of-runners that we knew who'd taken up this challenge, and as a bunch we'd welcomed two elementary school girls to our race, since they'd been upset about missing the kids' mile, a previous event in this local extravaganza of miling, a fund-raiser and memorial to an outstanding former runner at the school—Adrian Martinez, who had died tragically a few years earlier, right after graduating from college.

I was here out of various senses of obligation: I wanted to support the Adro cause, and was looking forward to touching base with many in the local running community who would be there to do the same. I had told the organizer, my longtime fellow cross country coach Steve Lane, that I'd come, and knew lots of other folks who'd surely be there, including my older son Patrick, a classmate, teammate, and good friend of Adro's. Furthermore, I'd sold myself on the idea of running this thing, of seeing how fast I could get through a mile, months before, as I mentioned near the end of Chapter Two. You could say all my training had been pointing to this thing for nine or ten months.

Well, had I actually *done* any training you'd have been able to say that. Unfortunately, and a major reason for my discomfiture on the starting line, I really hadn't trained at all. My fall plan, you may recall, had been to do a great deal of resting throughout the winter months, and there, I will say, I was true to the regimen. Day after day I tirelessly rested, no matter what sacrifices were involved. Hey, discipline is my middle name!

On February 11th, I had what seems to have been my heaviest "training session" of the winter. On a lovely walk around Great Meadows I broke into a trot for not one but *two* stretches, each lasting an entire song on my iPod, one through Dan Hicks doing "I Don't Want Love," about 3:45, and then a second a bit later through R. Crumb's "Hula Melody, that one actually almost 4:00. Yes, you're right—serious power funk hard-core training music this isn't. But the songs *are* lively and that helped, as did starting very slowly (and staying slow!). I loosened up enough in both cases, and got to trotting a tiny bit more freely by the end of both, helped by knowing the end was coming soon. Power to the iPods! Nearly eight minutes, in two rather extended stretches, of not-walking!

If I'd repeated that sort of day, tried to expand on it, adding a third trot, perhaps, or trying to push one of the trots up to reach, say, five minutes, I'd have probably progressed somewhat. But I didn't. That would have felt like moving into full training mode and would have required heading out with serious goals in mind three or four times a week, at least. And, through the winter, I couldn't bring myself to do that. This was my resting time, remember? The previous January and February I'd been recovering from my lung cancer operation, getting used to one-lunged walking at all, timing five-minute walks weaving through the furniture in our house. It was enough, thank you, that this year I was walking around outside for an hour a day.

I did get in five or six sessions, over the winter months, of cross country skiing. A couple were pokey squishy plods out through my back yard and around Great Meadows, but I also got in a few outings on groomed trails and did some free-style skiing as well as classic-style. An early-January, two-day visit to Woodstock, Vermont, was the ski highlight—one day I must have gone more than two miles on virtually perfect trails, with, I'll add, quite a few breaks to catch my breath. Pumping my poles, and "skating" a bit awkwardly but steadily, this was real freedom of movement and, best of all, at something like a real running pace. Beautiful and exciting. Leaning gasping on my poles I gazed ecstatically at the frosted line of pine woods on the hillside across the brook as I panted and readied for another go. Wonderful day—and rare!

Basically, though, day in and day out, there was no special training at all, just the daily walk. And on March 20, the first day of spring, rather than beginning my true training regimen, as I'd thought would happen when originally dreaming up my mile test, I left with Christopher on a cross-country driving trip of nearly two months. We were good about keeping up the walking, and missed only one day in the nearly eight weeks we were gone. But there had certainly been no training upgrade. I suppose I could say our weeks spent in New Mexico, living at 7,000 feet, constituted a sort of altitude training. I did in fact feel the thinness of the air on some walks, most notably on a trek labeled "easy" that in reality climbed from 6500 to 7100 feet high over a stony mile and a half. But easily outnumbering efforts of that sort were plenty of easy strolls along birding trails or seashores.

When we got back from our splendid drive, in mid-May, there was less than a month to go until the mile thing, which had been in July the previous year, but—in a change not good for me—had been moved up to June for 2010. I caught up on routine medical appointments, and also had to focus on some events around my official retirement from teaching, and furthermore I had another special pedestrian project, a marathon-length walk, that called for some of my attention. That necessitated setting aside a day in each of four or five weeks for building-up-to-mega-walks, days when I'd be pushing myself, but to go farther, not faster. I couldn't wait until the end of June, after the mile event, to start this stretching-out process or I'd be facing my marathon walk in late July or even August, and likely facing serious heat and humidity. It seemed patently unwise to plan harder training days more than a few times a week—back-to-back track and distance sessions? No, I rationalized, I wasn't ready for that, and so embodied a self-fulfilling prophecy of diminishment.

In other words, I'd blown it. As far as any true, serious training regimen sensibly orchestrating me towards real exploration of my one-lunged miling limits, I simply didn't have the time available, or so I told myself as June loomed. This was not completely true, of course. I could have made *some* time and made *some* improvement, but something kept me from it. Hard as this is to admit, there was something distasteful, now, something unpleasant, about these little effortful trots of mine. The inevitable gasping recovery was too visceral a reminder of my reduced capacities, seemed less a step to fitness than a depressing *memento mori*.

I've never been much of a swimmer, but grew up living near the ocean and always have swum a bit and always have felt secure in the water. I could in past years transfer my cardiovascular fitness from running to swimming slowly across nearby Walden Pond, for example, mixing my strokes to rest parts of me as I slowly swam. I had an embarrassing moment, however, the summer after my lung-removal surgery, when taking a family camp safety-check swim test. After three or four easy crawl strokes, I'd have to stop and breathe while treading water. Trying a modest backstroke, I could go a bit further but also had to rest. And even just treading water was, in a new way, an effort. I labored as the lifeguard listlessly noted my struggles on her clipboard, and loved it when I was told I could grab the ladder a minute early. My happiness at ending the ordeal was doused, however, when I was told I was consigned to the kiddie pool for cooling-off purposes, and forbidden to actually jump off the dock and swim with everyone else. Ouch.

Somehow I no longer felt secure in the water, and a kind of nervous discomfort came upon me when I felt myself having to breathe harder. I wasn't really, exactly, completely panicking, but was consciously stopping to rest before I got to that state. And in the same way, I no longer felt secure about pushing through a running limitation. When I began to get a bit breathy I couldn't simply slow down and keep going. I had to walk, in a sense to feel myself on dry land again, and had to let my panting and gasping fade back into normality.

With June's arrival, and no real training in place, I considered bailing out on the whole run-a-mile idea. But when I ran into organizer Steve on one of my retirement-connected visits to the high school, he urged me to participate, stressing the low-key nature of the event and the many rookie runners I'd have as company in the "newcomers' mile." I could be classed as a newcomer, he said, since 1.) I'd never run a mile in real competition in school, college, or thereafter, and 2.) my one serious mile effort, described in Chapter One, had been thirty years earlier. In the end, I swallowed hard and decided to go for it. I'd learn something, whatever happened. And thus I was on the line with my serious crew of competitors. And certainly I felt like a newcomer, in that I had no idea what to expect. I knew I'd have to do some walking to get through a mile, but how much? What would constitute a successful mile for me! Was time even relevant? What could a watch tell me about success? What would be a good mile for me?

I was excited, you'll recall from the first chapter, to have run a sub-five minute mile three decades earlier, to have run one mile about as fast as Bill Rodgers had run every mile in his wins at the Boston. Could I do one mile at a marathon pace today? OK, not a winner's pace, but an acceptable pace. A qualifying pace?

The current standard for men 65-69, my age, to enter the Boston Marathon is to have run a 4:15 (you can get in with a 4:15:59); this is an average of about 9:50 per mile. Could I run one mile under ten minutes? No. I might have been capable of a single lap of the track at about that pace, but that would constitute an all-out 400 for me now. Doing ten minutes for one mile seemed daunting, when my walking pace is about twice that. What about going *twice as slowly as my own best marathon time?* That was just under 2:45, about a 6:15 pace, so for that, I'd have to do my Adro mile in 12:30. Given that my previous experiments had yielded times around fifteen to sixteen minutes, that seemed a challenge. But maybe I could get there.

The real problem was, as usual, my ego: I harbored somewhere deep within me a desire to run a nine-minute mile and blow myself away. Heck, that was a bit slower than my regular training-run pace just a couple of years ago. Could it now be that hard? Well, yes. I knew, really completely knew, that that wasn't going to happen in these circumstances. I'd invested no real effort in improvement, and besides that, was still in the late stages of having had a cold, with a faintly detectable remaining wheeze on mild-ly-effortful occasions. And this occasion promised to be more than mildly effortful. Knowing I was headed out to whatever my limits were, I was, in fact, nervous.

Despite knowing that I wouldn't be able to run the entire mile, I took the event seriously enough to break out my old road racing flats for the occasion, and also tried a hit of ventolin as we left for the track, about for-ty-five minutes prior to the race, in case that made my breathing stronger. (Ventolin is albuterol, the inhaler mist used by various respiratory-challenged folks in distress; I'd gotten an inhaler from my pulmonologist before our spring trip, knowing we'd be at altitudes that could chal-lenge my lungpower.) For the event I'd decided that I wouldn't wear a watch. For one thing, there was a huge clock near the finish line so I could check splits easily, and for another, I didn't want to be bothered with the distractions of constant checking and figuring as I struggled along. I did want to give my best effort, however weak that might turn out to be.

It was a gray, coolish evening, perfect for miling, really. Our motley field was readying itself, and at the last minute, a fit-looking woman in her thirties jumped in, clearly destined to be our winner.

At the gun we were away, me dropping to the rear right away from the outside spot, Christopher plugging away in front of me and the kids and other grown-ups in front of her, the late arrival already well out front of everyone by the time we were around the first curve. That was about all I saw of the rest of the race, immediately focusing on swinging into my pace and visually concentrating only on the track a few meters ahead or so, looking up every so often just to see where I was on the circuit. My basic goal here was to maintain my trot through the first quarter-mile lap. Thereafter I would see how things felt. I jogged through in about 2:45, in fact, feeling pretty good, a pleasing surprise. Wow, eleven-minute pace! For about fifty meters more, I even wondered whether I could do another whole lap like that, maybe achieve a half-mile under six minutes. But by one-hundred meters later, after the curve, maybe halfway down the back straightaway, I decided not to gamble and walked for a bit, maybe 80 or 100 meters, recovering before, as I came around the turn up to the finish, picking up to my trot again, wanting to be running going through the halfway point and the largest clump of spectators.

And there *were* spectators. For the various miles — kids, newcomers, elite men and women, open men and women, masters men and women, and even scholastic miles—there were around one-hundred competitors altogether, and each had his or her fan club/support crew. Plus there was a vendor tent with shirts and other running stuff, officials and a results tent, bunches of kids from the track and cross country programs, some helping out, some just hanging—quite an audience, really, compared to my one practice track session two days ago, when there were one or two other runners or walkers and a small gaggle of ladies on towels doing their outdoor yoga class. Past the start area halfway along, I even heard a few "Go, Mr. Hart" cries. Naturally I forced myself to run through that stretch, but was trying so hard to keep focused on the track that I neglected to check my half-mile split. It had to have been a bit over, not under, six minutes somewhere, given my walking break.

I kept this second trot going for almost a full 400 meters, walking again, my second break, around the end curve before resuming my trot up the homestretch and past the start into the bell lap. The race had been won sometime during that third circuit of mine (the late arrival, as expected, took it in 7:00 flat) and as I started my final lap there was no one remotely close to me. My three-quarters split was probably a little over nine minutes. The girls and the middle-aged moms were streaming across the finish line as I plodded around into the backstretch. Christopher, I found out later, had slowed a bit to see if I could catch up to finish with her, but was almost a minute ahead of me going into her final lap. Aliya and Carina, my elementary-school neighbors, had the kindness not to lap me, but finished well ahead in 9:30 and 10:13, respectively. I wondered, drawing away from their happy finish line into my final lap, with 350-plus meters to go, if I should try to close all the way from there. I wasn't thinking about finish times as I considered whether to keep going or not, but simply whether I was sure I could get through the last lap without a walking break. My attention was all on my step-by-step, stride-by-stride progress.

My son Patrick, there for one of the alumni miles, had been urging me on from the inner side of the track, moving around on the backstretch to give me encouragement, and I decided to walk near him for a short stretch so I could finish with a "kick" rather than sputtering and risking having to walk my last one hundre meters or so. So I walked down to the final curve, then picked up the pace for a running (sort of) 200-meter close. Whether the crowd noticed, I don't know, but I certainly felt that my final stride was longer, for the last one hundred meters, perhaps, close to—gasp!—an eight-minute pace?! That final thirty seconds stretched itself into what seemed closer to a week. I didn't miss the clock this time; I was thrilled to push across, and more pleased than I'd thought a guy could be with a mile time of 11:45!

The organizers were pleased, too, in that they could then proceed with more of the miling events, and on the evening went, successful in providing thrills for everyone. The elite women's and men's miles were won in excellent times of 4:37 and 4:10. A 75-year-old woman, Mary Harada, may have had the day's best effort overall with her 8:11 mile, announced as an age-group record. While

I could claim the day's slowest mile, the Power Pokeyness Prize went instead to a ten-year-old who did three excruciating laps in his wheelchair (a heavy, non-racing chair at that) and won everyone's heart with his superhuman efforts. By the time he finished that third lap, after twenty hard-working minutes or so, every spectator was pulling so hard for him that our own arms were tiring.

By contrast, and despite hearing some encouraging cheers, I mostly felt fairly invisible during and after my race. I realized that the high school kids who knew me from my coaching days were not watching the Great Former Runner engaged in an ennobling quest, but instead were seeing a normal me much as I'd generally appeared to them, sometimes jogging but mostly walking or standing around. There were a few adults around who knew me and my story and who may have watched my effort with some thought, but most were doubtless like the local paper's sports guy, who approached me to ask about the event and get a quote about Adrian and some of the alumni runners present. As he questioned me about this or that, it became clear to me that he had no idea that I was working with one lung. He certainly wasn't interested in my particular effort; he may not have even seen it, or may well have been embarrassed to bring up such a stumbling, futile performance at all. I thought about that, and even started to explain my own effort, then gave it up, despising myself for the attempt. I had to accept that to most observers I was simply another out-of-shape old guy.

But still, my 11:45 both surprised and tantalized me. The three short walking breaks had definitely added time. I calculate that altogether I walked for roughly 250 meters and, if I walked them at my usual walking pace, that might have meant a little over three minutes. Had I been able to "run" continuously, had I jogged through them at my opening lap's pace, I'd have saved about 1:20, for an imagined continuous mile time under 10:30.

Later, I reflected that, building on this, I could realistically perhaps aim to get down near ten minutes—after all, I had done virtually no training, and that last tantalizing 100-plus meters suggested that perhaps I could be incorporating more of that sort of pace in my training, if I actually forced myself to train. I had felt my lingering cold making me wheeze my way around— surely without that I could have been a bit quicker? A minute faster, maybe more, seemed eminently possible, incorporating some training at the quicker regular running pace. Yes.

But no, I reasoned. Why do I need to make a 10:30 or 10:00 mile a goal? Can't I just close the book on my miling career at this point? Well, sure, that's easy enough to say. But what about having no running goal at all? Is that what I've come to? The bottom line here is that, unlike many of the other running experiences I've written about, which usually left me scratching my head as I sifted through a *smorgasbord* of various possible ways of understanding them, this mile effort of mine has a very clear message for me: I'm basically no longer a runner.

And that made, and makes, me very, very sad. Do you run? I used to.

CHAPTER NINE

My Good-bye Marathon

A man must find his occasions in himself, it is true.

THOREAU, *WALDEN*

BACK TO GOOD EXPERIENCES, WITH one of the best, my life's longest walk (to date, anyhow). In the end, the epic walk fell a bit short of providing a sample of every possible sort of walking, but was wonderful nonetheless.

T he halfway point of any marathon is a good time
to assess how things are going, though these on-
the-fly assessments can be treacherously tricky.
Boston marathoners in particular know the seductive
surges of power one can feel cruising invincibly through
midpoint Wellesley, and how those same siren surges are
sometimes regretted a few miles later, in the Newton hills.
My self check-in at the halfway point of my last (most
recent *and* final) marathon told me I was doing reasonably
well. Yes, I could feel the accumulating miles a bit, but I
was comfortable, breathing easily, legs feeling OK. Better
than OK, in fact. I was seated happily in a Lexington,
Massachusetts bistro with a delicious slice of pepperoni
pizza in my stomach and the last remains of a cold pint
of Sam Adams in front of me at the table. It was noon,
and my 26.2 mile walk had begun a little before 7:00 that
morning. I would be moving along again soon and probably would be done before 5:00, marathon accomplished.

Okay, okay, people—bear with me here, please—yes,
I am talking about *walking* a marathon. Walking the marathon distance, that is, twenty-six point two miles. Silly,
I know. Hours and hours. Don't worry, it won't take that
long for you to read about it.

And I don't want to hear any grumblings about my
lunch break. Here I was simply following the example
of serious long-walk predecessors, who were not averse
to taking breaks along the way. Ancient Mariner Samuel
Taylor Coleridge, celebrated British poet, critic, and
party talker of two centuries ago, on a walking tour
of Scotland in 1803, totted up some 263 miles in eight

days—an average of about 33 per day! True, at thirty, he was less than half my age, but he already suffered from numerous physical complaints (mainly some painfully debilitating forms of gout) and was hitting the opium pretty hard, so we can't exactly count him as some extraordinary physical specimen or as being in the bloom of youth. Sam took his time, as for instance on September 4, 1803, when he left his inn (after a hearty breakfast) just after 8:00am and arrived some thirteen hours later (9:00pm) at his destination, had tea, and went to bed. At my roughly twenty-minute-per-mile meandering pace, he could've covered nearly forty miles that day, though he does mention a mid-day break during which he "sits on a grave stone to write about the experience." I also presume he ate somewhere along the way, resting there. The point is, he could walk all day, with breaks. I had decided to allow myself equal privileges during my effort, and had indeed practiced the same marathon day lunch on my preparatory twenty-miler ten days or so earlier.

Yes, I was walking a marathon, and why not? If the mile is the universal coin of the running realm, the marathon is surely the most widely-known road race distance. There are over 100,000 marathon finishers a year in America today. Tell someone you're a runner and you'll likely be asked *Oh, do you do marathons?* Ask a randomly-selected passer-by to name a road race or an Olympic distance race and you'll likely hear the word marathon.

It wasn't always thus, and a quick look at how the marathon came to be so prominent offers a fine example of Unintended Consequences. (I *will* make it quick, and I'll ask you, meanwhile, as I digress, to imagine me walking and walking, post-lunch, returning towards my home-town Concord, now along a shady, paved, bike trail.)

In 1969, after seeing the field for April's Boston Marathon top one thousand runners for a second straight year, the Boston Athletic Association announced that in 1970, if one wanted to run in their annual twenty-six miler, one had to have run a previous marathon in a time of four hours or less. Will Cloney, Jock Semple, and the other reigning Guys of the B.A.A. (I capitalize Guys to emphasize the male-ness of marathoning at that time, for the first official woman's division wouldn't arrive at Boston until 1972) doubtless thought they'd put a lid on that little overcrowding issue. The runaway growth they'd seen would now be brought under control. *Mission accomplished.*

Sorry, Guys. As a means of limiting the race's field, the policy was a miserable failure. Despite ever-toughening standards (they cut a half-hour off the qualifying time, down to 3:30, in 1971, went to 3:00 in 1975, and then 2:50 after 1979 for men under forty, for example), fields grew rapidly.

The 100th anniversary Boston Marathon in 1996—the last marathon I *ran*, after emerging from a marathon "re-tirement" of over a decade to qualify in a 3:30-ish time the previous fall as a fifty-year-old—had a mind-bog-gling 38,708 official entrants, and some 36,788 starters. There were a reported 35,868 weary finishers, of whom I numbered myself among the very weariest, stumbling in in around four hours. (My chip time, I believe, was closer to 3:45, but even that was over an hour slower than my best for the distance, and, despite that, a lot more painful.)

Despite their entrance-requirement strategy's failure to curb growth, Boston's curmudgeonly organizers should be congratulated for the far-reaching effects of their ruling, which coincided with the arrival of world-class marathoning in the U.S.A., and was a huge factor in American distance running improvement. Boston fields are now a bit smaller (the 2010 edition had a mere 26,736 official entrants, for example), but that's much more a function of the availability of so many other excellent marathon opportunities around the country than it is a sign of reduced marathon popularity.

Runners are like everybody else in at least one respect: what is made inaccessible to them is also made more attractive. Getting into Boston, once qualifying standards were set out, certified a runner's competence, so more runners were pushing harder in more races to make the grade. Now there was a recognized level of achievement to which a runner could point and say "I made it." Boston Qualifier races sprang up all over, and what had been a handful of marathons nationwide quickly became a full schedule in every region. Boston is not even the biggest marathon any longer; several cities boast races that vie for that honor. New York's mega-event, once a cult-status multi-loop Central Park trot, had some 37,899 entrants in 2008, for example, while Chicago 2009 claimed 33,475 finishers.

Now, in 2010, I was going to "make it" to the conse-
crated distance again, but walking this time. Yes: I was
indeed compelled by the desirability of the unavailable.
Being short a lung doesn't create day-to-day living problems for me much at all. I walk, ride a bike easily, play
golf, can do some cross-country skiing in the winter,
and so on. Recently retired, I can always find time for a
walk, and get out for about an hour every day. Decades
of running helped me, even in my mid-sixties, make a
solid recovery from the cancer surgery, and resume regular activities relatively quickly. But my most regular
activity, my daily run, was denied to me. I resented that,
and wanted to push back against that denial somehow. If
running twenty-six miles and change, back in the 1970's,
had made me feel like a "real" runner, had been a center-
piece of my running and planning and training for years,
couldn't I at least now achieve that distance, if not at the
same pace, again? I was being reminded, all too forcibly,
of the inevitable diminishment and loss we all must face
sooner or later, but I wanted to focus on what I *could* do
rather than what I couldn't. Long story short, I was walking those 26.2 miles because I couldn't run them.

Of course beyond that angry motivation lay plenty of
other reasons to think an all-day walk would be a good
experience. I was ninety-five percent sure I could, physically, do it (keep going and sit down when you get tired,
right?). I'd been walking about an hour daily and my
marathon ramble would afford me ample opportunity to
think about how that basic life routine was coming along

as a running replacement. It would be a day of discovery and celebration, set aside as a gift to myself, like my 37-mile run day on my 37th birthday decades ago. It would be special, and it would be. . . yes, it would be fun!

In the end, I undertook the Walk with the goal, consciously spoken or not, of investing the experience with enough specialness that it would force me to pay attention. By its scale, it would include virtually every sort of event, internal and external, that can happen in a walk. Emerson examined what he called Representative Man. This would be—tah-dah!—the Representative Walk. If I wanted to understand my walking, the need for it, the satisfactions derived from it, the problems and or threats generated by it, a marathon-sized walk fit the bill just fine.

So rejoin me now on the bike path, please. I'm the shortish, ordinary-looking guy in the cargo shorts and baseball cap. The one glancing nervously upward at that persistent cloud canopy. Hmmm—was it actually going to get rainy? Had I been a fool to reject Christopher's offer, for my return walk, of an umbrella she'd thoughtfully brought to our lunch meet-up? I was a couple of hours from home. How would those hours, and miles, go by if I was, well, wet? That might not feel so good. And how good *did* I really feel right then anyway? I had definitely stiffened up somewhat as I sat for lunch, and felt tight and rusty as I worked to warm up again. Worked. Was that it? Was this going to turn into *work*? In the perspective which defines work as the absence of choice, since I had little choice now but to keep walking, did that consign this effort to being actual *labor?* And not only labor, but four or five more hours of it!? I wanted to walk my twenty-six miles, not labor through them.

To shake off those gloomy speculations, I tried to refresh myself by recalling how splendid I had felt five hours earlier, as I emerged from the woods that border our back yard and turned right to walk out along the main causeway of Concord's Great Meadows National Wildlife Refuge on a gloriously crisp blue July morning. My shadow was thrown a good thirty feet ahead of me on the grassy path and the early-morning sun warmed the back of my neck most pleasantly as I proceeded.

There was virtually no one about; I'd left home at ten before seven. I'd given a distant wave in the direction of a fellow readying the Great Meadows mini-truck for the day as I passed the refuge's workshed, and had exchanged a few happy superficialities with an old gent on a side trail just off the main loop as he sat taking huge-lensed pictures of a bunch of wood ducklings peacefully paddling with their mom. That was the extent of my human contact for the early in-town loop of my journey. Even when out on a road accessible to cars (for perhaps fifteen minutes of my first eight and a half miles), there was little or no traffic.

I'd decided to begin the day with a local loop, cutting through Great Meadows to Monument Street, then crossing the Old North Bridge, drawing inspiration from Emerson's lines about embattled farmers and the Shot Heard 'Round the World. I'd wander some walking trails and generally be in shaded woods. The morning was brisk enough (under sixty when I started) that I wore jeans and an undershirt for those early miles. A couple of hours later, crossing an open field before returning for an at-home pit stop, I was glad to shed one shirt, though it was closer to seventy now, nearing nine o'clock.

Coming back through Great Meadows, I could hear the boinkings of bullfrogs and the raucous trillings of redwings and around them the rest of the day's ambient whistlings and burblings. Thankfully there was not much in the way of whining mosquito buzzing. I'd get through the morning, I imagined, spend much of the mid-day on a paved bike path where mosquitoes weren't common, and be back home, happy on my screen porch, well before the serious evening armies of evil bloodsuckers emerged.

It had been a little bit threatening to feel, just over an hour into the walk, a kind of twinge going on with my left foot-strike. Nothing, really, except as I thought about seven or eight more hours of pounding the pavement, I realized that I couldn't take any physical signal lightly. Running a marathon, for an adequately trained runner not concerned about a fast racing time, shouldn't be depletingly arduous. When I was running several a year, only a couple—my fall Boston qualifier and then Boston in the spring—were all-out efforts, and I can remember pacing someone one year to a 3:15 race in what was basically just a long workout for me. Of course, then I was half my present age, and regularly putting in 55- to 60-mile weeks. Training to run marathons was something I at least knew about, therefore, even if I no longer was running them. But was I in fact adequately trained for my marathon this time? How in the world *does* one prepare for a nine-or-ten-hour *walk?*

I'd never been a serious hiker or walker. Who had time, after all, when running daily? Many runners are essentially indolent, and, aside from their miles, have little time or energy for exercise of other sorts. My own reading, strumming, gaming and watching habits, certainly, are not aerobic. Probably the longest I'd ever walked was five or six hours clambering up and down well-trod New England mountain landmarks like Monadnock or Moosilaukee. I'd be out there for three or four hours longer than on any of those climbs on my marathon, sort of like tacking one ordinary marathon run time onto a six-hour walk. How, again, does one train for that?

I had warmed up to it, extending the length of my longest walk each week or so from the more or less regular three miles to seven, thirteen-plus, and finally a little over twenty. This was in the six or seven week stretch following our return from a cross-country driving extravaganza trip on which Christopher and I had congratulated ourselves on simply getting in a walk of close to an hour almost every day. Our longest on the trip was probably only about four miles, but at least we were very regular. If I huffed and puffed quite a bit on canyon walks at 7,000 feet, so what? That wouldn't be the case strolling at sea level at home. One part of me knew, or thought it knew, that I could probably just do the marathon-length walk, taking breaks as needed, without any preparation whatsoever. Another part cautioned that anything taking so much more time than any previous walk had to be treated carefully and with due respect.

And I did learn a few things as I pushed out the length of my long walks. The first extension happened without any planning at all, as I simply extended my usual walk from an hour to two one day. I'd gone out feeling good, and just decided *en route* that this would be a good day to go a little further. I learned on that particular walk that, out for several hours, I'd have concerns about going to the bathroom. I learned that having a cell phone wouldn't have been a bad idea. That building in a couple of breaks for snacking as walks got longer would likewise be sensible. And, facing my wife's irritation when I returned, that letting other people know what one's plans are is a must.

Other people.

Let's admit it: there is something fundamentally selfish in any serious runner's approach to the activity. I certainly didn't ever object to running with other people, and plenty of times found joining up with some others for a training run or a particular workout to be helpful and fun. But when I was putting in the work to train for marathons, getting the miles in was the prime consideration, and that often meant squeezing in a run before work, or on my lunch break, or perhaps as part of my commute. And mostly this meant running solo. Even when serious marathoning was behind me and I was doing half my previous mileage, fitting those thirty or so weekly miles into working and parenting and my whole life meant grabbing them when I could, and again doing solo fit-around runs most of the time.

What turns out to have been the case is that the aloneness of those runs was as important as the getting them in at all. The (roughly) an hour a day on my own, pulled away from family and work, was a needed break, as important mentally and spiritually as it was physically. I'm a reasonably gregarious sort of fellow, and enjoy socializing in many forms, but I also need time on my own, time to myself. And my running was basically all of that kind of time I ever got. It was in fact, expressed wordlessly, an insistence upon having such time.

Walking, much more than running, is perceived as a pleasant social activity. One of the main benefits of having walking rather than running as my daily exercise is that it's much easier for my wife to join me. We rarely walked together in my running days. This was not only because my runs were tailored to specific training purposes, but also simply because time was at such a premium. It's easier for most groups to accommodate to each other's walking pace than for random groups to run at the same tempo. It's easier also to say to guests at our house *let's go for a walk around Great Meadows* than it is to say *hey, let's go run five miles.*

On the other hand, I need time alone, too. And somehow if I was going to do a Walk grand enough to be both spectacular and representative of all my wayward remaining pedestrianism, then that walk had to be a solo. On my second lengthening walk, a thirteen-miler, we arranged that I'd drive over to Lexington early one morning, park, then walk back to Concord. There I'd pick up Christopher at our house, from whence we'd return, walking back to Lexington for lunch and an easy drive home. But for the twenty-mile trial extension we merely met in Lexington for lunch, and that was the plan for the actual Marathon Walk, too. (Though I'd be passing through the house in mid-morning and mid-afternoon and thus getting to check in with her then as well.) I'd be on my own for the day, essentially.

Of course, for much of the day I'd be walking on a bike path that would have plenty of activity, but there I felt invisible most of the time, and certainly most folks walking, blading, running, or biking along weren't paying much attention to me, or to each other. In the way that each marathoner in a race has his or her own unique experience of the event, I'd be walking alone. I sat briefly on a bench as I got to the paved bike trail in Bedford early in my second morning stretch, wondering a bit about the next phase of my marathon and the people I'd inevitably share space with. As I sat wondering, I suddenly noticed there was a new sky going on. It featured a vast low layering of gray masses, puffy and shelf-like and dark, except for a few scattered gaps into the bright blue beyond, which in places revealed blazing white sunlit cloud-piles in a dimension beyond the dark canopy. Wondrous, really, but potentially nervous-making, too. Those were the same clouds triggering tiny tremors of trepidation post-lunch. Well, until the rain came, I thought, might as well enjoy the shade and relative coolness from the clouds.

As it happened, I basically lucked out. The day never got hotter than low 70's, there was cloud cover from the middle of the day on until I was done. Had I planned the walk for a day or two later, I'd have had to pull it off during a stretch of drought-ish weather that saw record heat and area prohibitions on outdoor water use. The knowledge that serious heat was coming had pushed me to set a date, to make the warm-up walks happen, to get this thing done. Here's where the Marathon Walk was just like previous running marathons: it called forth from me an absorbed fascination with the weather. Any marathon (or ultramarathon) calls for such devoted attention, because these events don't happen all that often. Confirmed Boston Marathoners know how tragic it is to plan a whole year around one day's run, and then have that day turn nasty, even to the point sometimes of obviating the event's competitive viability. At the Athens Olympics in 2004, no one expected record-breaking times in that heat, and yes, all the competitors had to fight the same conditions. And what a great race it was for medalling Americans Deena Kastor (bronze in 2:27) and Meb Keflezighi (silver in 2:11), even though their times weren't at all their best. But when it's not so much about competing for medals and instead focuses on adding one more precious Boston to a limited life list, it's a shame to see weather conditions define one's performance more than training readiness. Jack Fultz was surely happy with his pokey 2:20 win in the Boston Broiler of 1976, but many of that year's sub-3:30 qualifiers had to be depressed by times significantly slower than their dreamed-of Boston bests.

My legs loosened up pretty quickly after lunch, and though they were getting somewhat tired and had pretty much lost their morning spring, they weren't generating any real calls for my attention. Oddly, it was my *hands* about which I found myself more conscious. They were both swollen, puffed up and tight-feeling. I'd noticed on my very first longer walk that after my usual hour of walking, whether because of gravity or the constant swinging motion, my hands got swollen. I didn't think this dangerous, but it caused a nagging awareness. With fifteen-plus miles accomplished, I literally couldn't pull my hands into a fully fisted position, my fingers were so fat. Even my forearms grew and felt tight, pumped up as they might be after a weights session. I had noticed the effect even more in my thirteen-miler, and between that and my twenty-miler I mentioned it at a visit to my doctor, who didn't see it as a danger. I should add that she had a positive but generally under-whelmed "Oh, that's nice" sort of response to my noble walk extensions and indeed to my projected epic walk. In this way she was nicely representative of most people.

My hands are slender, with visible bones, tendons, and veins, but by mid-walk they appeared as smooth balls when I tried to close them into fists, knuckles unnoticeable on round, meaty mitts. But unnoticeable was the proper word for all of me, really, walking along solo as the afternoon produced more and more bikers, joggers, bladers, and walkers. The condition of my hands, indeed of all of me, was of no interest to anyone but myself. Folks had other things to think about and fortunately, so did I.

For example, had an hour passed since lunch, and was it therefore time to flip on the tunes once again, after giving my iPod a rest? I always feel just a twinge of guilt when walking with earplugs beaming tunefully. They can have the effect of helping to envelop me in my own world, where I doubtless pay less attention than I should to what's going on around me. Mindful awareness and Thoreauvian grokking of my world are desirable, yes, but must we not equally allow for the beneficent influences of, say, Ella Fitzgerald's transcendent rendering of the Duke's *Sophisticated Lady* with its wondrously breathy Ben Webster sax solo? Tunes *could* be considered as energizing fuel, and thus as belonging to Thoreau's stratum of basic necessities of life. (The four he lists in the long first chapter of *Walden*, "Economy," are Food, Clothing, Shelter, and Fuel.) Certainly they provide energy, whether via Steely Dan's *Kid Charlemagne* spot-on guitar wailings or the Roches' gentler if equally ironic *Hammond* harmonies. Each person must, of course, step to the music which he hears, however measured: if you want Fifty Cent in your head or the Berlin Philharmonic, blessings on you either way. The bad part of listening while one walks is that one can become lost to one's surroundings and rapt in a musical mist. And, of course, that's the good part, too. To plug in for your walk or not to plug in is a legitimate debate. Many would agree with Gregory McNamee, who blogged on Brittanica.com about the vast benefits of walking at all levels, then said "You're disqualified by the way if you walk with a mobile phone or iPod in tow." Uh-oh, here I was breaking both rules on the same ramble! Luckily on my mega-walk I was spending so many hours perambulating that I allowed myself the luxury of being on both sides of the argument, albeit at different times.

Today there are road races at which iPods are banned, the claim being that they represent, in a crowded running environment, a potentially hazardous distraction. My main marathon-running days came before technology made running with sound practicable, but by my sixties, when I was pushing myself in shorter races for age-group geezer glory, I was equipped to try racing wired-up, so to speak, a few times. Problems can ensue when the question shifts from whether to listen, to what's on the musical menu. I orchestrated just one race playlist, for a five-K effort, and I can now see why. What can I have been thinking? I mean, sure, Chuck Berry's *You Can't Catch Me* seems reasonable, but what were tunes like Jackson Browne's *Running on Empty* or—no matter how toe-tappingly irresistible—They Might Be Giants' *Withered Hope* doing there? In retrospect, it's clear that I'd known inside I was unlikely to break 20:00 in *that* 5K! I never made another race playlist after that one.

Besides, for this day-long Marathon Walk effort, wouldn't my iPod simply die along the way somewhere, out of juice? What might then be the effect on a tiring walker as his equipment deserted him? I decided I'd put together a list good for around four and a half hours, a time I was sure my pod would survive, and that I didn't need to worry too much about fine-tuning it, just including good stuff I wasn't tired of.

And that indeed turned into a pleasant marathon-prep task. A little bit of everything, and a marvelously absorbing hour gazing at my laptop iTunes screen. I'd have some designated quiet times and otherwise listen when I felt like it. I ended up tuned in for about half of my trek. And I will say that I came away from the experiment with a more firmly understood commitment to walking podless with some regularity.

From the high school in Concord where I taught for many years, it's a short, easy walk to Walden Pond, and my American Lit classes usually spent a period making the trek with me to see Thoreau's original house site, which, among other things, features a large pile of stones to one side, a cairn built up by contributions over the years from many visiting pilgrims. Frequently kids in my class tossed on contributions of their own, and when we talked about the heap, I'd tell them about the incredible discovery, when the pile was cleaned up not long ago, that one lucky workman made: he found Thoreau's iPod!

Long thought to have been lost, the moss-encrusted device, I would tell them—once Apple technicians were able to get it to function again—would offer considerable insight into Thoreau's musical predilections and, by extension, his whole thought process. I mean, it's pretty clear, isn't it, that the fellow who used to sit and play his flute across the pond of an evening wouldn't have spent hours every day walking around the woods without his earbuds working, right? Henry was a listening kind of guy. *Much is published, little printed*, he tweets to us in the "Sounds" chapter of *Walden*. The kids then, as an optional extra credit assignment, could make up a playlist of what Henry was probably listening to, explaining his choices by showing their relevance to Thoreauvian principles and passages, and submitting to me a CD with their explanatory liner notes.

Thoreau comments on the freshness of household objects seen outdoors: ". . . so much more interesting most familiar objects look out of doors than in the house. A bird sits on the next bough, life-everlasting grows under the table, and blackberry vines run round its legs; pine cones, chestnut burrs, and strawberry leaves are strewn about. It looked as if this was the way these forms came to be transferred to our furniture. . ." Anyone who plays an instrument can experience this delight by taking his or her music outdoors and listening to its new qualities. Thus, too, for me to listen to my mixes as I walk is pleasant.

So I started up my pod again an hour after lunch, and arrived back home for a final snack-and-changing break just after 3:00. Mine was not a rugged, desperate trek, after all, but one on which I pampered myself shamelessly. For my closing phase, I swapped my somewhat limp shirt for a crisper one, and, more important, went with fresh racing socks and a switch to my old, ultra-lite Saucony road racing flats. I enjoyed some quick chocolate chip cookies and cold delicious milk, and, when I left this last pit stop with almost twenty-two miles behind me, I felt confident. Just four and a half miles more, two loops around friendly, familiar Great Meadows: these were clearly do-able.

And do them I did. As the afternoon lengthened, the familiar trails were dutifully trod; I use the adverb advisedly, since there was more duty than magic step by step. I savored the overcast day's mildness, relishing the temperate air, but was almost grumpy that no rain had materialized to make my ramble more objectively epic. Knowing now for sure that I was going to complete my quest leant tiny shadows to my self-congratulation.Had I aimed too low? Had I been too easy on myself? Almost ten hours had elapsed since I'd begun, and no brass band had materialized, no medals were on offer.

Shortly before 5:00 I had a shady sit for a final few minutes on one of the benches that are spotted around the reserve's main causeway loop. Frost's dictum is that a poem begins in delight, and ends in wisdom. My walk began before it began really, in the delights of anticipation and planning, and then took actual shape in the delights of the brilliant morning sun-slanting light on the blooming paths around Great Meadows as I walked through a basically empty Concord. The delights, in fact, were of every stripe, from idly watching the river flowing gently beneath me as I crossed the "Rude Bridge" near the Minute Man statue in the clear morning to savoring this final shady sit-down.

Yes, delights aplenty. But where was the wisdom? My calves were tight, and my feet felt draggy and just a bit pinched. They were surely a bit swollen by then, too, though not as much as my hands. I was glad to sit, both to get off my feet and to take a moment to consider the day, something I'd been pretty consistently not doing for several hours. I'd lost the thread of the day's specialness somewhere, or rather, I'd forgotten to pay attention to it. I was just walking along, after all. Having had no cosmic revelation, what had I missed along my not-so-very-epic way?

Yet the mild disappointment I was feeling, I realized, was more generated by the impending End of the Walk than by some dimly-registered lack of specialness. To leave my bench and finish the walk was to return to the mundane daily tasks of my "real world" existence. If nothing else, I had at least succeeded in walking so far into miles of mindlessness that pulling out of that state was vaguely undesirable. And I *had* walked far, indeed. Whatever hadn't happened on the mega-walk, and even without an event-commemorative t-shirt, the miles accumulated couldn't be denied. I was now a walking marathoner, and I trumpeted the fact to an empty living room on my arrival home.

I'm still mad about not running. The marathon memories my trek jogged loose for me may in fact have made me even angrier about what I've lost. But I do feel I've extended my walking range, and have added choices to where I go with that. It's certainly a lot easier now for me to say something like, "Let's walk [the thirteen miles] into Cambridge just for fun." Adding choices is the important principle here. Even the smallest of choices establishes a qualitative difference. So *the knowledge that I can decide to spend a day walking* is the needed boost at least as much as the day's walking itself. I'm saying, to my body, to the world, as a regally-postured toddler might angrily proclaim to a too-directive sibling: *You're not the boss of me!*

My last marathon was, simply, an active assertion of my ability to choose. I paid attention to the weather, to my iPod, to the possibility of an amazing oriole caught in a green leafiness, to my puffy hands, to speculation on pit stops, to my companions of the road and to whatever caught my interest. But most of all, I *chose* to take the time to pay attention to these things. That my attention wandered, dwindled, and malfunctioned regularly did not detract from the effort's ultimate value, nor did my inability to immediately express a wise moral of the adventure.

Here I side with Hazlitt, who relished long walks, especially solo ones, proclaiming that "I am for the synthetical method on a journey, in preference to the analytical. I am content to lay in a stock of ideas then, and to examine and anatomize them afterwards. I want to see my vague notions float like the down of the thistle before the breeze, and not to have them entangled in the briars and thorns of controversy." And here I would expand controversy to include not only debating with a companion of the road, but also the need to find a meaning at all. So, if I haven't quite rejected Frost's formula, at least I've offered it in a radically re-balanced version, heavier on the delights and fuzzier on the wisdom, which may, in this particular case, have simply devolved into the wise pleasure of soaking in a hot, deep, post-walk tub.

Years of thrusting Thoreau at high school students have taught me that, while many groan at wading through *Walden* as a whole, most respond enthusiastically to isolated sentences and pronouncements of our famous local literary curmudgeon. They happily hold out nuggets of his glittering thought, for example, when I ask them to find a sentence that most completely expresses the ideas of a chapter, or to choose a thirty-second snatch to read aloud on our pilgrimage to Thoreau's cabin site, and these thoughts genuinely move them. And when, as students will, they challenge me to do the same, to isolate for them a favorite Thoreauvian thought, I most often steer them to Chapter Two ("Where I lived, and What I Lived For") where, nestled into one of his many calls to awaken, he makes a wonderfully comprehensive announcement. I'll give the two lead-in sentences from there before the biggie:

> *We must learn to reawaken and keep ourselves*
> *awake, not by mechanical aids, but by an infinite*
> *expectation of the dawn, which does not forsake us*
> *in our soundest sleep. I know of no more encour-*
> *aging fact than the unquestioned ability of man to*
> *elevate his life by a conscious endeavor. . . . To*
> *affect the quality of the day, that is the highest*
> *of arts.*

To affect the quality of the day! Tantalizingly vague, and obviously of critical importance. Was my walk a success? Was it done well? I know this, at the very least: my mega-walk, my last marathon, surely (and for the better) affected the hell out of the quality of that July day. And beyond that, of course, as I soaked in post-walk bliss, my tub was warmed by what any runner, or walker, holds dear: I had a new PR, my pokey but proud good-bye marathon.

CHAPTER TEN

GREAT MEADOWS
GALLERY

For many years I was self-appointed inspector of snow
storms, and rain storms, and did my duty faithfully....
THOREAU, *WALDEN*

WALKING OF TODAY, NOT AS a substitute for running, but
just plain rambling around doing it.

F airly recently retired, I find myself asked the standard questions: "So what do you do with your
time now that you've got so much of it?" In various translations, they're asking, *What explorations, what
fresh directions do you find yourself taking now in this new
flowering of the retired life?* The sad essence, coming from
non-retirees, is more or less this: how do you justify your
existence? I have several thematic answers, but none may
fit the essence of that question, in its truest and best cu-
riosity, better than this: I make, and observe, small piles
of rocks.

In the spirit of Thoreau's unpaid work as "inspector
of rainstorms" for our mutual hometown of Concord,
Massachusetts, and "keeper of its wild stock," I have
lately found myself the curator of a small museum, open
to, if not paid attention to by the public. Many of the
works on display, I have to admit, are my own, but I have
my fellow artists.

This museum—really I suppose gallery would be a
more modest, and fitting, word—is scattered over the
acres that comprise the Great Meadows National Wildlife
Refuge, which extends out past our back yard, and has
long been my basic place for daily ramblings, walks of
an hour or so's duration. Noticing one day a couple of
unusually pleasing-looking stones along the main causeway path around the refuge's largest pond, I thought they
deserved a better chance to catch someone's attention.
I put a little group of them on a flat-topped low rock
along the path, where their smoothness and rich color

variations showed together to good effect. Suddenly the poet Wallace Stevens stole into my head:

> *I placed a jar in Tennesse,*
> *And round it was, upon a hill.*
> *It made the slovenly wilderness*
> *Surround that hill.*

My pile wasn't a jar, not something fully man-made, but rather a man-made construction of the natural. The effect, however, was similar: My obviously-artificial construct seemed—to me at least— to lend to the surrounding woods or rocks a new dimension. Its clear *intentionality* made it different from its setting, and changed the nature of the setting itself in turn somehow. At the least, it pleased me, and, I thought, might have given a pleasant ripple to the awareness of anyone recognizing it as a small human contribution to the scene.

My impulse here was not unlike that of seven-year-old Annie Dillard, as she relates it at the beginnng of her marvelous essay "Seeing," Chapter Two in *Pilgrim At Tinker Creek*. She describes her excitement, as she would place a penny somewhere "at the roots of a sycamore, say, or in a hole left by a chipped-off piece of sidewalk," thinking happily about "the first lucky passer-by who would receive in this way, regardless of merit, a free gift from the universe." I, too, could not help imagining my little pile catching some walker's eye— *hey, what's that?* The impulse to leave a sign of one's passing is surely not uncommon.

Recently my wife and I hiked up Mount Champlain in Maine's Acadia National Park. I'd assumed a modest 1,000-foot "mountain" was, well, the quotation marks give away my insubordinate attitude.

I, too, could not help imagining my little
pile catching some walker's eye.

Hard clambering it was, though, for me at any rate— Christopher's rowing fitness kept her strong, but she was working as well. I established a deep and warm relationship along our arduous way with the many (forty? more?) cairns, marker rockpiles on the ascent. Part of this was gratitude that we had some demonstration of progress towards sitting down and eating our limp sandwiches, but part was also the perfect niftiness of most of these artfully-placed shapes. Most were three large-ish granite chunks (fifteen or twenty pounds?), two supporting the third in bench-like fashion. I gratefully tested the sittabil-ity of a few. On some was placed a fourth, smaller rock, an addition that sometimes leant them a distinctly turtlish aspect. The proportions and configurations again imbued an intentionality that was in contrast to the extravagant wildness and vast views of our climb.

> *The wilderness rose up to it,*
> *And sprawled around, no longer wild.*
> *The jar was round upon the ground*
> *And tall and of a port in air.*

Over the walking months (most of the year at Great Meadows, though with a few periods of impassibility in the winter or at spring flood-times), my piling impulses led me to leave a dozen or more of my creations around and about. One successful "installation" seemed to call for another. What did this all mean? Was I a real artist, my increasing number of piles representing a growing *oeuvre*, or was I simply a ranging canine, marking his territory? Calder or coyote, it didn't, of course, matter. I might, in a day's ramble through the place, notice one or two of my piles, or a dozen, or none. But I did know generally where my creations were, and knowing that gave a certain new shape to my mental map of the refuge. I already knew the woods and paths well, but a new, almost-proprietary di-mension crept into my relationship with the place.

My additions to the Refuge's natural appearance gave rise, inevitably I suppose, to wondering about other in-stallations. What if, instead of suddenly noticing an artful heap of small stones, one saw, oh, say, a plump, inch-high, golden Boddhisattva figurine perched on a tree stump eight feet off a woods path? What new dimensions of meaning might be granted any number of *tschotzkes* now gracing various nooks and desks in my house? The urge to Put Stuff Outside, which called up great remembered pleasures from my childhood, still was powerful within me. The smell of mint growing all around the stone wall where I placed toy armies on long-ago summer after-noons came back to me. . . .But the idea of this, seductive as it was, also scared me and seemed problematic. What if a number of folks decided to enhance the Refuge's beauty with their *objets*? Some—horrors!—might not demon-strate my own obviously impeccable aesthetic sensibility!

My additions to the Refuge's natural appearance gave rise, in-evitably I suppose, to wondering about other installations.

My sole introduction of a man-made object, and one about which I had very mixed feelings, even came to regret, was the Q-tile episode. The tile, special of course by virtue of its being one of the five letters of which each Scrabble set has only a single one, I set Dillard-like into a richly green, mossy spot at the base of a pathside oak. It lasted there no more than a couple of weeks. It was not a glossy plastic competition-quality ProTile in an eye-catching color, but a dark wood tile from a standard old set. Its disappearance gave rise in me to various possible scenarios of its being noticed and then removed. I mean, after all, one would always pick up a noticed piece of litter, wouldn't one? Can't have people dropping things, leaving things, throwing things away. Beyond simple neatness and environmental responsibility, though, there might be at least the question as to whether or not the finder/remover was a scrabble player, even perhaps with what degree of seriousness? Then, too, one remembers tales of jays and magpies and other corvids picking up stray baubles to embellish nests.

However it disappeared, the original "art," the installation, as it were, no longer exists. Good-bye, Q-tile, and bless you whether you're in a drawer, forgotten, tossed away in some garbage dump, or maybe even resting back among your fellows in a Scrabble tile bag. I can almost see it— a game with two Qs suddenly, what seismic shifts in the Normal World. The "art" has life, though, in that it's been replaced by exactly these speculations of mine. One would say that this shift to an existence only in my imagination has rendered that public art work a private one, though it now has also a private life in the imagination and stories associated with it by whoever found it, too. And what if that finder, in turn, showed the tile to someone else, with a laugh, later? The ripples of story might spread, a butterfly-wing-changing-the-world effect.

That Q was, in any case, an aberration—my entire body of work otherwise consisting of my simple piles. Some grew to as many as six or seven constituent rocks, and once I had a few in place here and there, other locations seemed to beckon to me regularly as possible grouping-worthy spots.

Some grew to as many as six or seven constituent rocks. . . .

My recent year's-end accounting had me noting just over twenty groupings, but the number is fluid. I've been delighted on occasion to find a new sculpture created by someone else. Two lovely piles, each of three smooth, flattened ovoid rocks, dark but of pleasingly contrasting earthtones, I noticed one day about five feet to the right of a woods-path I walked along, up four feet or so above ground level on a natural shelf on the side of a protruding boulder. What excitement! Crusoe discovers a footprint! I've re-stacked these when the piles have dissolved, by whose hand I know not, extending my curatorial duties to all works in the gallery, not only my own.

Another example of someone else's creativity came in mid-August, when water levels had sunken down very low. Walking in on the main causeway, over the last footbridge area headed back to the main parking lot, it was so dry I didn't need to take the footbridge, and instead walked right across the concrete blocks that form the bed of the dip that sometimes is a channel streaming from the west side of the causeway to the east side—and there I noted the big rock blocks that spread out from the west side. And *zap!* That's where I saw a lovely work of museum art, a clearly human intention: seven of the black dead water lily clusters, looking like strange dried shower heads, were lined up in an arc, one each atop a line of rocks. One could have conceivably been left on a rock by the vagaries of wind and water, even a couple. But this graceful parade of shapes had to come from someone carefully laying them out one at a time down the line. I loved it! By the next time I passed that spot a few days later, a storm had passed through and the pods were gone, scattered into the masses to be found clumped at the base of the reeds that edge the ponds or in piles along the side of the path. That "art" probably existed only for a day. It made me think of Andy Goldsworthy's wonderful natural-object mega-structures, many purposely designed to eventually dissolve in currents of whatever kind.

And yes, I surely know that the real art, the Great Art, at Great Meadows is wrought by nature's hand, not mine or any other human's. A beautiful September example was the astonishing feat of the spiders. The morning had begun with a sort of fog—the previous day chilly and damp, this day much warmer, though it took the sun until after 8:00 to break through the mists. Tomorrow would be the fall equinox, and the seasons lately had been alternating days, a summery one followed by crisp autumn flavors, then back to warmth. The spiders had been at work overnight, and for virtually the entire length of the causeway's east-west axis stretch there were dew-bejeweled delicate complete webs, dazzling in their intricate architecture. Some were quite small, only two or three inches across; most seemed closer to half a foot. There were as many as seven or eight on some of the high plants—blue vervain, I thought, seemed to lend itself best, but I saw webs on everything out there, jewelweed, evening primrose, ancient loosestrife, meadowsweet, sometimes even strung from one plant to another, though more often limited to one. I was lucky and happened to be there at exactly the right time that morning, as the sun had just broken through and the moisture hadn't dissipated. A glorious gallery of glistening artistry. Charlotte's Web for as far as the eye could see, its message unwritten but clear as the morning: not *Some Pig!* but in this case, *Some Day!*

It wouldn't have been a wasted morning to watch those webs disappear. Already some were torn: surely the bumblebees left around couldn't be captured by these gossamer nets, nor the many early-fall goldfinches and other little perchers with their own errands in the neighborhood. And who knows? Perhaps a studious watcher would be rewarded by the actual sighting of a spider! Their total absence from the splashy display was, to this amateur at least, conspicuous. By this evening, would these masterworks all be gone? Could some big ones survive longer than a day? The biggest I saw was probably over two feet top to bottom and more than a foot wide, 22 or 23 radial divisions and as many tree-ring widths. But no spider was on it anywhere, nor could I see one curled up along a stem or leaf sleeping off its exertions or admiring its own handiwork. Could the creators have already harvested any morning crop and retreated to their living rooms to read quietly?

Early this past spring—mid-March?—I was thrilled to see a small tumble I recognized as having been some handiwork of mine from the previous fall on a wide stone along the pathside on the main causeway loop. Broken up though it was, the notion that it had in any form at all survived the snowy winter gave me a warm feeling. No weavings of mine would ever rival the masterpieces of the spiders, but I had an edge in staying power, whatever that was worth.

But art is emphatically not eternal. Many of my efforts I've been perfectly content to lose to winds, varmints, or whatever fate there is that doesn't like a pile. In the few cases where my handiwork has been associated with another man-made structure I never made any curatorial efforts at restoration once time took its course, having come to be dissatisfied with that juxtaposition of human intentions. One little group hunkered down at the base of one of the railing supports around a new viewing platform lasted for nearly a month—its chief virtue was that I could make it out from back on the main path, gracing its little corner plot. Another small grouping on the concrete pedestal base of a viewing bench lasted quite a while before disappearing. But the proper distance between the natural and the artificial had not, somehow, been maintained, and this sort of thing I generally view now as a failed experiment.

Most of the time I can stroll past piles simply observing, but there are times when my curatorial urge compels me to tidy up the bunch in some way. Once in a great while, I can see evidence of someone's having noticed my work, generally by seeing that it's been altered in some way. One long-in-place pile became, suddenly it seemed to me, a line of rocks instead, artfully curved. My excitement was, I hope, some variant on the excitement of others who might have noticed my original piles. Communications from other civilizations!

Though it's a year-round gallery, seasons naturally bring changes. It's most open in early spring, though there are high-water periods that limit access.

Though it's a year-round gallery, seasons naturally bring changes.

As the plants along the path around the largest pond grow higher, the constructs are at times obscured, even at times made invisible by the luxuriant burgeoning loosestrife, evening primrose, milkweed, and other lush growths. This too pleases me, as I like the idea of the piles going into hiding, as it were. When the water does get high, and I occasionally wade through places where the path is flooded, it's a treat to sometimes glimpse one of my piles now under a few inches of water. Not many folks will notice completely-submerged creations! This seems to me to amplify the reward granted by the universe (to use Dillard's construct) to the perceptive wanderer whose pilgrim eye drifts onto it.

I diverge from Stevens in the end. His final stanza overemphasizes negatives and the artificality of the jar. Rock piles do not behave the same way, certainly never

"taking dominion," and (I hope) being describable, however modestly, in terms more positive than "gray and
bare." Stevens concludes with an emphatic, if famously
cryptic, assertion, while I avoid considering any conclusion at all.

> *It took dominion every where.*
> *The jar was gray and bare.*
> *It did not give of bird or bush,*
> *Like nothing else in Tennessee.*

Supposing my walks to have some exercise value, my
curatorial duties can be fitness-frustrating, forcing me to
make stops along my rambling way far too often, whether
to re-group a disintegrated pile, to snap a photo, or simply
to admire a friendly little heap again. I try to accomplish
this just in passing, but sometimes need to slow down or
stop to really look for a pile. Sometimes I look in vain,
finding nothing where I knew I'd had something in place
before. It's always interesting to speculate on how my mag-
nificent artworks disappear. ("My name is Ozymandius,
king of kings,/ Look on my works, ye mighty, and despair.") I imagine sometimes a gleeful knocking-down by
a toddler, sometimes an oblivious swishing-past of a fat,
wet muskrat. I myself would never dismantle an intended
pile, but I guess there must be those who do. I console
myself for disappearances by realizing that in order to
disassemble something, one generally must first notice it.
Thus destruction is at the same time recognition. (Less so,
of course, in the case of critters or the elements.) I noticed

just the other day that an installation of single stones atop a bouquet of sapling-stumps had been swiped clear, after what had been a couple of months of obvious existence. I moved on past, attempting no restoration, and, truly amazingly to me, noted the piece had been rebuilt by someone else the very next day! Now I was channeling Saul Lewitt, reveling in someone else's re-creation of my pattern. Free Art, it's for everyone!

. . .truly amazingly to me, (I) noted the piece had been rebuilt by someone else the very next day!

I worry occasionally about obsessing too much...is it in fact possible any longer for me to walk around Great Meadows without slowing, stopping, peering, searching, assessing, grooming, placing? Luckily, the answer is yes. And I consider that what I lose in fitness benefit I make up, to some degree at least, by attention paid. Walking

can't be only a fitness activity after all; it has to be associated with sibling-word *waking* as well, being awake to
the world. By making any construction, I become more
a part of the scene; I do so equally by noticing them. My
piles are little alarm clocks of a sort, calling me to wake,
and possibly, at best, even nudging some others into a
thoughtful or pleasurable noticing.

And that's enough. On the title page of *Walden*,
Thoreau places under a line drawing of his little woods
house a quote from a later chapter: "I do not propose
to write an ode to dejection, but to brag as lustily as
Chanticleer in the morning, standing on his roost, if only
to wake my neighbors up." In this sense, I needn't be entirely ashamed of my modest curatorial efforts, and of my
confession to being, in my retirement, a maker of piles.

CHAPTER ELEVEN

THE ART OF LOSING

My thoughts go to sleep if I sit still. My mind does not work if my legs do not shake it up.

MONTAIGNE

SO, AM I NOW A runner, an ex-runner, a walker, or what? How, exactly, does my pedestrianism define me—or not? The conclusion I come to here both surprises and pleases me.

Velocity, expressed as $V = S(r) \times S(l)$. That is, speed is calculated by Stride (rate) times Stride (length). A simple formula, useful in some coaching situations. A simple way to understand, or enter into a discussion of, running style and biomechanics, for example. Simple, and misleading as well, in that it might appear that since running and walking can equally be measured by this formula, they are the same. But they're not.

In 2007, my third year of training hard enough to be competitive in my over-sixty age group, my knees had started to ache by late summer and I'd backed off. Then cross country coaching starting in August led into the school year, when I was especially busy, resuming duties as department chair. I ran a bit through the winter, cross country skied a bit, and was content to postpone any resumption of serious training until summer of 2008, when my quest for geezer glory would continue.

I raced only once during the spring of 2008, at the Lexington five-miler on Patriots Day, mainly to keep older son Patrick company. We lined up at the very back of the field, and I wore training shoes and an iPod to remind myself that, though I'd won the over-60 division in this race the previous three years, this time around I had no such ambitions. I ended up mildly disappointed to have finished on the wrong side of forty minutes (40:11) but glad to have actually done the race at all. It was a good reality check, I told myself, because I'd assumed (wrongly, of course) that I could pretty easily get under forty minutes with some minimal pushing over the last mile or two.

Mixing biking days in with running, I hoped to be able to keep my growing-balkier knees from malfunctioning as I regained some fitness, and still thought I could get back to better racing form for the races I'd key on through the summer. In early June I made a bad snap decision to spin around and go after a tennis ball lobbed over my head by younger son Eamonn, taking a fall that badly separated a shoulder and left me in a sling and a non-runner for a few weeks just when I'd counted on starting to really train. I had to miss my beloved local July 4 five-miler and, ominously in retrospect, my training log was ignored, showing no entries after June. I went though July and August just not feeling like racing somehow, my running remaining flat and lifeless.

I remember an early-September run in 2008 with a recent graduate (one of my best-ever cross country girls) around the high school's cross country woods, showing her the new 5K course. The course features plenty of ups and downs, and my main bodily memory of that day is of me huffing and puffing. Embarrassed to show my weakness so much, I was happy to pause here and there to assess how a certain section would play out for race strategies and to compare the new layout to the old one, whose record book was basically a recap of my companion Cassi's four-year career. I put down my struggles to being out of shape, and also thought the low-level, persistent cough I'd been experiencing ought to be checked out when I had my physical the following week. Possibly I had some sort of respiratory issue, bronchitis or something.

Instead, not many days later, my wife and I were in a pulmonologist's office, looking at computer images from a CT scan that showed a good-sized tumor throbbing in my right lung. Once diagnosed with lung cancer, I am sure I must still have run, but not so very much. The next three or four weeks went by in a tense, speeded-up blur of preparation for unplugging from my various teaching, coaching, and department chairing chores, as I knew I'd have to be away from those for an extended period— months, if not the rest of the school year. I know I must have run a few times, but can't recall any details of what had to be wedged-between-things pokey trots of half an hour tops, whether from school or from home.

An exploratory mini-operation less than a month from the diagnosis led to a plan for a couple of months of chemo and radiation and then a January 2009 lung removal. During chemo and radiation I was content to walk rather than run, content to "stay active" in that way, and to congratulate myself on simply getting through my toxic therapies without being flattened. I was pleased to get to both the EMass and State cross country meets, watching the girls get second and ninth. When winter closed in, with an operation looming, I know there were days I never got outside at all, content to "rest up" from my therapies in the weeks leading up to the operation. Plenty of nice pre-and-post-holiday reading.

I remember some December and early-January snow, and getting in a few days of easy cross country skiing. Fun, again accompanied by the rest stops I associated with simply being out of shape, or, I'd by then acknowledge, with being sick, which I felt, as always, was temporary. I really don't think I ever thought *soon I will not ever be able to run any more.* Denial? Was it simply, literally, *inconceivable* to me that I might be *unable* to run? I'd accepted a defining narrative that I'd "deal with" the cancer and then return to my normal life, back to teach for my long-planned final year eight months after the operation. I'd beat this stuff and get back to the Plan, back to my regular good old teaching and coaching and all of that. Wrong again, Tom.

Lost somewhere in my memories of those hectic months is whatever turned out to be My Actual Final Real Sustained Run. Was it clumping around Great Meadows, or just jogging into town and back on Bedford Road? I don't know. I am not a fellow who harbors regrets, but I admit that not being able to recall the last "real" run of my life is painful to me. I preach paying attention and celebrating the ordinary, and I blew it on that one, and it's not something I can fix.

I remember waking last December to the first real snowfall of the year—only an inch or two around here, but still the true blanketing of white. Through the morning a windy swirling continued even after the snow stopped, and then the sun emerged and the day turned gloriously blue, while temperatures climbed to a comparatively-balmy mid-to-upper 30's. Walking around Great Meadows was wonderful—not ski-able really, but snowy enough to compare critter tracks of various kinds, including shoeprints of the eight or ten intrepid trekkers who'd preceded my mid-day circuit there. I almost felt a tad overdressed, sensing the sun even through my layers.

And just thinking about layers reminded me of the coming full winter. Thoughts of bundling up. Heavy thoughts. Booted plodding. We had had enough bitter, sub-freezing days already for me to have seriously missed running's ability to truly create a personal, portable heat environment in winter. To be warmed up and running easily is a treat at anytime of year, of course, but especially so when the rest of the world seems to be clumping lumpily under layers of dumpy down and heavy wool. No, walking and running are not the same things at all.

I don't exactly wish to make the claim that running made me a grown-up, but I know its arrival in my life coincided to some degree with my reaching that state of being. I started running regularly rather late, right after I turned 31, and I only became a grown-up in my early thirties as well. Became a grown-up, that is, as in

coming off of automatic pilot to make conscious deci-
sions and choices about my life, as opposed to drifting
into grad school and early teaching and even a marriage
in my twenties because those were the things one did.
I made no deeply-considered decision in 1966 to go to
grad school and become an English teacher. Doing those
things meant simply following the paths of least resis-
tance and general acceptance. Indeed, I bailed out of
teaching in 1970 for a fifteen-year self-granted sabbatical
basically because I knew that I wasn't yet a grown-up,
was more like my students than like my colleagues.
Running I *chose*, bodily and consciously, when I did,
because it made me feel good in so many ways. My wife
of over half my lifetime shows up in a few cameos in the
foregoing pages. Can it be altogether unrelated that I
began my running practice the same year I met her?

When I ended my sabbatical and returned to teaching English in 1985 (luckily enough in a wonderful high
school where I could enjoy a fruitful, quarter-centu-
ry-long career) being a parent and having worked in the
grown-up worlds of bookselling and publishing made
real teaching possible for me. But having plugged through
nearly a decade of running by then, including plenty of
marathoning and racing, also helped me in the classroom
in countless ways.

You can't misrepresent yourself running, or at least
can't in the sense that you can't not train and then go
out and run a marathon. You see your true self in your
running, even if at times that self might be one you're not
comfortable about seeing.

A small, somewhat humorous, early instance of this came to me in 1976, shortly after I ran in the first Ocean State Marathon in Newport, Rhode Island. It was also my own first marathon, as it happened, and after completing it in a little over three and a half hours, behind only about three-quarters of its (for then) huge field of several hundred, I was mighty pleased with myself.

Never mind that I'd had to walk some. Never mind that I was stiff and sore for days afterwards. I had crossed an important line, and felt I was somehow now a different, a more legitimate, runner. I saw myself in a new light.

But only until I really *did* see myself.

A woman with whom I'd shared some miles at Newport (until she pulled happily away a few miles from the finish) sent me a copy of a picture someone had taken during the race. There was Karin, all right, and there next to her was. . . oh no! *That* was my shining hour?

Jaw drooping, eyes glazed, my inspirational tee shirt (*Secretariat, Super Horse*) flapping languidly on my weary (and embarrassingly wide) body, there I went, my spindly legs emerging from baggy red shorts in what appeared to be an ordinary, if somewhat stiff, walking gait. I looked to be of human origin, but only distantly. Recovering to race again after that picture shattered my illusions about how I looked while running was tougher than the actual physical recovery from the race itself.

I recall years ago when my plan to run the commute back to my Somerville home from my downtown Boston office met a snag. I'd forgotten to bring in with me my pack of running clothes! I had an old pair of running shoes there, however, and ended up doing the seven-mile trot home perfectly happily in my khakis and an only semi-buttoned dress shirt. I looked idiotic, totally un-runnerly, but after feeling awkward for the first mile or so I decided not to care about that. When I arrived home, about an hour later, I was sweaty and bedraggled, and had a new understanding of the practicality of normal running apparel. But I'd also had a lesson in the silliness of thinking I had to look "runnerly" in any special way while running. No one had hooted or hollered or poked fun at the guy running in long pants and a dress shirt. Basically, I'd made it home unnoticed, abandoning my own self-consciousness along the way.

I think of these things now, when most running that I do is done in my regular walking-around clothes, lumbering slowly along for a couple of minutes, perhaps, bundled (in December, say) in a winter jacket and my flannel-lined blue jeans. Somehow I can't truly feel like a runner when I'm dressed more as though I'm a spectator at an outdoor hockey game. But—*Earth to Tom*—the fact is I'm not a runner any longer.

Among other losses, losing my running means losing a most convenient way to describe myself. Not only could I say I was a runner, but I could say at any given point that I was, for example, a 2:45 marathoner, or a competitive senior division five-miler. I could offer numbers as identification: I ran thirty miles a week, or ran every day. I had been running for twenty years, or thirty years.

Quantitative change I can accept gracefully: my days of marathons in the 2:40s are long gone, and that's OK. My 27:13 five-mile PR will never improve; I knew that more than twenty years ago. That's OK, too. My 33:27 for five miles at sixty—though equally inaccessible to me today—gives me an equally warm glow. Five miles of steady easy running, at any pace, is as remote from me as a 2:45 marathon now, and as I hit 66, I can't quite put a similar value on my five-mile walk that takes me over an hour and a half. Something's simply gone. Quantitative change has turned into qualitative change. Running has become an entirely different thing: walking.

It's not just that walking is slower than running. And it's only partly that my current form of pedestrianism is no longer central to my day, something I plan around. (Though I'm glad to report that the regularity of daily walking has me out there just about every day, whereas even when training about thirty miles a week, I'd miss a day or two weekly.) Walking isn't really, in the sense that running and racing can be, and were for me, a self-worth-boosting, ego-lifting external validation. I have no cool commemorative t-shirt to trumpet my walk around Great Meadows yesterday. No, walking's not this, it's not that, it's not that other thing either. So, what is it?

Walking can't simply be understood as Not-Running, in the same way prose can't simply be understood as Not-Poetry. In a Thomas DeQuincey passage Thoreau copied into one of his own commonplace-books (one classic walker admiring the writing of another), the author of

Confessions of an English Opium-Eater is expostulating on Herodotus being called the Father of Prose. DeQuincey says "If prose were simply the negation of verse ... indeed, it would be a slight nominal honour to have been the Father of Prose. But this is ignorance, though a pretty common ignorance. To walk well, it is not enough that a man abstain from dancing. Walking has rules of its own the more difficult to perceive or practise as they are less broadly *prononcés*."

But if walking has rules, they must be pretty easy to follow, because literally everybody walks. Nothing to it. Who doesn't walk? But while we all walk every day, perhaps we can't all say we *go for a walk* every day. That's the move from walking as part of the need to perform any activity (shopping, say) to walking as intentionally-chosen recreation. Maybe it would be more precise to say I'm a daily recreator. Therein may lie the all-important capacity, that choice to re-create.

At bottom walking is, for me, in this sense of chosen recreation, in some unbudgeable way, *necessary*. And much good follows from that. I know on my walks, as I did on my runs, that what I'm about is all I need to be about for that time. I am not pulled in any direction by any obligation other than putting one foot in front of the other. This is all I am doing.

Much of the time, for most of my days, that is not the case. We humans are multi-taskers, and whether we do that poorly or well, most of us read the paper over breakfast, or do e-mail while watching baseball—oh, and better just pop into the next room quickly between innings to move that laundry into the dryer. Oh, and while I'm up it makes sense to take the chicken for tonight out of the freezer. . . . doesn't it?

As a teacher I was constantly juggling things— moving a class through its paces, from the quiz returning to the homework-modeling to the discussion of this or that passage in *My Antonia* to reading another passage aloud to steering a student's attention back to what we were about to answering a question about— and so on. And that's the way one had to work; that very juggling, artfully done, is how effective teaching happens. But it's great to have a break from the need to multi-task gracefully, to have a chance to forget everything but your breathing and moving.

And breathing and moving and being outdoors count for a great deal, after all. My practice of walking is in its way my flesh-and-blood journal, and it is as mundane as a journal, too, though at times I can spice it up with consciously-paid attention. After all, isn't it possible to find—incumbent upon us, in fact, to find— the sacred in everything? *When you know how to listen*, it is said, *everyone is the guru*. Walking, one does reflect; one has made time, and time enables reflection.

I can recall a certain scorn felt by me and by my regular running comrades during the boom years of the late 1970s towards those who went on about the Zen of Running and described the *satori*-like experience of "the runner's high." We felt that one ran not to find enlightenment, not to find bliss, of whatever sort, but simply because one ran! To ascribe any sort of collateral benefit, mundane or sacred, to the activity was, however implicitly, to admit a need for justification, a need no true runner would ever feel.

Running needs no purpose but itself, and it is in that spirit that I want to embrace the purposelessness of my walking. Yes, I realize that it's exercise of a sort, but aerobic training-wise, my ambling isn't significantly different than walking a round of golf. While a few extra endorphins may sluggishly clamber from their glandular recesses into my active brain while I walk, playing a sloppy but happy, up-tempo *Ain't Misbehavin'* on my guitar probably does at least as much for me in that line.

I'm simply choosing to be a walker and, as noted in previous chapters, it's all about choosing, about the ability to make choices. Every walk I take is a validation of my capacity to choose, whatever its particular circumstance or purpose. I miss running as much while I type these words as I ever have, but I identify myself as a walker now, not a runner. I run a bit now and then if I want to get warmer on a cold outing, and I might run from one viewing point to another to check the progress of a cross country race I'm watching, but sustained running of any kind isn't on my plate anymore.

The art of losing isn't hard to master, said Elizabeth Bishop, and the past couple of years has given me some practice in that line, and as I wrap up this book, it's clear to me in a new way that it's about loss, but about compensation as well.

If my daily run has become my daily walk, that's not entirely a bad thing, is it? Walking . . . running. . . running. . . walking. First I ran, now I walk, and I juggle and debate between the two, counterpointing my past and my present pedestrianism in ways productive and, well, not.

Flash forward a day or two from these wintry musings. After a day so relentlessy gray and blow-away blizzardy that I actually didn't set foot on any sort of a walk outdoors at all—it happens, sigh—I go forth into a late-morning vault of bright blue over a foot-deep, snow-bound, welcoming, sunshiny landscape. I'm wearing my gripper-tread-add-ons stretched over my snow boots. Floundering into Great Meadows I pause to chat with a trio sending an eerie screech-owl sound from an iPhone gizmo app crying into the surrounding woods. The usual tree hole is empty, though, and only jays are currently curious about the little iPhone's shuddering cries. Leaving this group, I press on, trying my best to be mannerly and avoid stepping in the ski tracks that have been grooved into the edge of the snow-filled roadway by what must have been several cross-country skiers by now.

With the snow at mid-calf in places, I'm feeling really stupid for not having put on my just-received present of some nylon/fabric gaiters. These are just the conditions for them! Still, the snow's pretty dry, and my flannel-lined jeans are holding up fine. When I can, I try to use the Yeti-like tracks left by what must have been an early-traveling pair of snowshoers. Sometimes I'm simply flopping through on my own, and I remember how effortful snow-walking can be. Plunging unevenly through a virgin stretch onto another woods trail, in fact, I'm not walking at all, really. I'm, I'm—what should I call it? I seem to be clambering.

Clambering! That's it!

In this moment of floppiness, alone in these winter woods, it comes to me, my long-overdue glimmer of wisdom. Today is every day, and yes, the day is the epitome of the year, thank you Henry, thank you brilliant snowy today. You've taken me off the hook and shown me the ridiculousness of my false dilemma.

Today it doesn't matter if I see myself as a runner or as a walker, because today there is no question that one can only *clamber*, which is neither running or walking, but instead a relatively effortful and unbalanced lurching sort of progress along hardly-marked ways. Life, exactly! I clamber on, step by wobbly step. I pause a welcome pause and extend my arms in symbolic embrace to the woods spreading out around me. I know now that it is exactly and always *clambering* that is what I do, who I am. What better way have I really to describe my progress today, or my progress anywhere along my meandering life of choices good, bad, and indifferent? I claim clambering, and may I not offer it to you as well?

Surely we are all of us clamberers, whatever the season. Cross country clambering, in fact, all weather, all terrain, just as the time-honored motto says on the state meet t-shirts. Days differ only superficially, and through them, in whatever vagrant mood or (in)capacity, we clamber. Is that you, in the shadow of those trees? Look. I'm right over here. Join me, and power to the pedestrians!

EPILOGUE

I have some good news and some bad news, readers. The good news is that not long after finishing what you've just clambered through, I ran a continuous mile that was a bit faster than the one I'd done in Chapter Eight. And did it without track workouts or arduous training runs, did it despite the same lack of running-workout preparation that undermined my Adro Mile effort of the year before.

Credit where credit is due: it was my wife Christopher's fault. She had taken up rowing, and we found ourselves with a high-concept erg (rowing machine). In trying it out, I learned that I could row, more gently than she did, for longer periods than I could run. I could row 500 meters in under three minutes, and extend that to 2000 meters in the mid-eleven-minute range. I liked this, and began to think it could be a useful regular form of exercise. Then at a regular doctor visit, when my vital signs were being taken as usual, I noted that my heart rate, which my walking kept at a mid-day resting level of about 70, maybe a little higher, was now at 64. There are always variations. I'm a guy who's in enough doctors' offices to get his vitals recorded quite a lot, but that got my attention. And my attention liked the idea of getting into some form of training, as I was looking at a second cancer surgery, this one a radical prostatectomy. What we'd been stalling on since 2009, a couple of biopsies later, had upgraded into something I didn't think I could afford to continue to simply wait-and-see about, however watchfully. My wife pointed out to me that in fact it might be the case that I'd be told I was not a good candidate for surgery, being after all a 66-year-old with one lung. So I was thinking fitness. . . .

When I soon thereafter rowed 3000 meters (in something like seventeen minutes) for the first time, I decided to check things out. I grabbed an old pair of running shoes, pulled on shorts and a t-shirt, drove over to the track, parked, walked over to and got on the track, then without further warm-up, ran a mile, four times around without stopping, in just over eleven and a half minutes. My solo effort I timed at 3:00 for each of the first two quarters, saying to myself "If you can row for seventeen minutes, you can trot along like this for twelve." As I finished my third lap, I noticed that I'd picked up my pace to a 2:54: I had warmed up a bit. From my 8:54 three-quarter check I pushed through the final lap in 2:43 for an 11:37 mile time. Oh Yeah! In Your Face, Mr. Can't-Run-a-Sustained-Mile! For good measure, after some walking resting, I pushed through a 2:08 single-lap quarter mile. Boo-Yah! It's all coming back! Erg Power!

OK, there's the good news. The bad news is I can run, but I'm not really running. I didn't spend decades running so that I could test myself and see how fast I could get through a mile, and I wouldn't want to run daily if my runs were all like that triumphant but arduous achievement. It was in the end simply another reminder that running is more than measurements of whatever kind. $V = S(r) \times S(l)$ may enable you to break down to understandable math a mile run and determine that you went at a five-minute, or maybe a ten-minute pace. But there's no comparable R-equals formula able to express what running is in that objectively measurable way.

The wonderful, multidimensional part that running played in my life is not going to be re-created by my going out each day to grind out a timed mile or learning how to gut out a mile and a half, or two miles or three. I can't be thinking with every step about pace and what's left in the tank and how near I am to my own red-line state. That's not how I want to run! Yes, running sometimes demanded pushing myself, and I loved that, finding out what I could do. But that important piece of the totality of running can't become all of what running is. I want relaxed runs as well, I want sustained pleasurable trotting, I want—whoops, back to quoting, and this time the Stones, correctly pointing out that we can't always get what we want.

Well, what if I could train up to achieve a sub-ten-minute mile, and then could run easy twelve-minute miles? That would qualify as running, not walking, certainly, and might be enjoyable enough for half an hour, say 2.5 miles, once around Great Meadows or Fresh Pond or the like. Is that doable? I don't know. Am I going to find out? Maybe yes and maybe no; I reserve the right to wait until I come back from my prostate surgery to decide that question. But is it at least nice to have that question out there? Yes!

It's nice because it hints at possible choices I can still exercise—yes, the power to choose, an affirmation of life! And it's nice because it highlights again, here at the end of this tome, the subtleties surrounding the walking/running dilemma, the balancing act of loss and compensation we're all engaged in all the time. Nothing ends, clambering continues, perseverance furthers. Pay attention! Running, walking, clambering: we must always be alert to the possibility that we have already succeeded.

About the Author

Tom Hart was a contributor to *Marathon and Beyond*, as well as to other running journals including *Runner's World, New England Runner, The Runner, Running Times*, and *Yankee Runner*, as well as to John Parker's ultrarunning anthology *And Then The Vulture Eats You*. An English teacher at Concord-Carlisle (MA) High School for 25 years, Hart ran his first marathon in 1977 and his last in 1996 at the 100th Boston. He also coached the school's girls cross-country team, and was named *The Boston Globe's* cross-country coach of the year in 2004.

Hart was born in Mt. Kisco, NY, graduated from Greenwich (CT) High School, and in 1966 from Trinity College. He also earned a Master of Arts in Teaching from the Harvard Graduate School of Education. His life in the book business began at the Harvard Book Store where he became manager in 1975. He was a sales representative for Random House, then paperback editor at Houghton Mifflin; there he edited the company's poetry series, bringing into print such poets at Baron Wormser and Tom Sleigh. In 1986, he edited the GK Hall fiction series, reissuing in paperback works by well-known authors such as Mavis Gallant and Francine Prose.

In 1983, he started his own literary agency, Thomas S. Hart Literary Enterprises, which he managed for the rest of his life. He represented authors such as naturalist John Janovy, sportswriter Peter Gammons, essayist and novelist Luis Urrea, novelist Alan Hewat, and young adult fantasy novelist Amelia Atwater-Rhodes. His clients also included runners, coaches, and running writers such as Marc Bloom, Don Kardong, and Steve Scott.

Hart shared his love of American literature with his students, often taking them to Walden Pond to discuss the works of Henry David Thoreau. He viewed the writings in **First You Run, Then You Walk** as ruminations on running and walking in the company of his favorite authors, among them Montaigne, Hazlitt, Coleridge, and, most of all, Thoreau. Hart saw Thoreau as a model of the attention we must pay to our daily activities. Of himself, Hart said that he had been "fortunate to live and work among books all his life."

For four years after Hart was diagnosed with lung cancer and had his right lung removed, he continued to run, walk, write, travel and follow his cross-country team.

He lived in Concord, Massachusetts with his wife, poet Christopher Jane Corkery. His three children —Eamonn, Patrick, and Rebecca—continue his life's work of running, walking, writing and teaching.

Tom Hart died in December of 2012.

CPSIA information can be obtained at www.ICGtesting.com
Printed in the USA
BVOW04s1458170714

359436BV00003B/1/P